RICHES WITHIN REACH:

A RETIREMENT CURE

KENNETH BRISTOL

Kenneth Bristol

Copyright ©2023

DEDICATION

To my father, the late Lauriston Bristol;

my mother, the late Elizabeth Ann Benjamin Bristol;

my Siblings, Olivia, Diana, Lauriston Jr, and Laura;

my sons, Johnathan, Kenneth Jr, and Keyeric;

my ascendants and descendants;

and my church family.

INTRODUCTION

Hello. I am Kenneth Bristol. My hope is anyone who reads this book will find something of value to enhance their life. Disclaimer: I am not a tax professional, lawyer, or financial advisor, and I'm not financially or politically motivated. I am not a guru on any topic. I am a person who feels intensely compelled to share what he has learned. I come from humble beginnings, and one of my most cherished wishes is that my message becomes bigger than myself. I pray this material touches enough hearts that my craving for learning and sharing lives on in others long after I'm physically gone.

The information in this book is not designed to be a solution to any one issue. Rather, it is a seed planted in faith that others will find something within these pages that sends them down a path that ultimately improves their lives.

This book will help readers discover their "next step" to their Riches Within Reach. The goal is increasing one's personal development, resulting in the formation of multiple streams of passive and residual income and creating a legacy to pass on to future generations, all while establishing a successful retirement.

Although I advocate business ownership and self-employment, having a job is not the end of the world. Properly done, a job can fund business opportunities, provide stability, and be a learning ground for expertise in any given field. Having a job has many advantages if you treat yourself like a business. Hopefully, you caught that last part— "Treat yourself like a business."

I am aware that many 'gurus' and people on the Internet are scammers. I, too, have made choices to follow many entrepreneurs and joined a ton of programs that promised financial growth, success, and even wealth beyond my wildest dreams. Of course, these were sales pitches, and it didn't happen.

That said, I want all to know that those same programs planted the seed necessary for the growth and success that I have been blessed to enjoy. Every opportunity, program, and training course I've been involved with has taught me something. I learned something from each and every one, even if it is what doesn't work. My financial success didn't happen until it was supposed to, not when I wanted it to.

I do not hold any individual or company accountable nor give credit to any individual or company for my failures or successes. That glory belongs to my Lord. All I have and don't have, and all my achievements and failures, are simply the accumulated results of all my own decisions and indecisions. I owe my success and failures to the Most High, to whom I pray, as I believe His mercy and grace allow me every thought and feeling in my mind and heart.

I am aware that we all want success in our lives. Conversely, I'm sure they exist, but I believe only a small percentage of people live their lives to be miserable on purpose, but that's another topic. I also believe that success means something different for each of us.

Some feel their life will be successful if they properly raise their children to be happy and fulfilled by their standards. Others believe success is paying their bills on time. Others may feel success in life is not being in credit card debt. Still, others may judge success based on the status quo of society, meaning going to college, having a career, getting married, buying a home, having children, and growing old surrounded by grandchildren.

Success is a feeling, a status, a self-determined definition of happiness, and we all want it. A good question is, what does success look like to you? In the end, what determines if your life was a success? Who makes that determination? Do we go on to glory easily and quietly, or do we fight for another day because there is "one more thing" that we just "have to do?"

I have heard the statement, even heard songs referring to the end of life, and it begs the question, if we died today, did we live a full life, a satisfying life, a life without regrets? I agree with the many who believe a life worth living is a life without regrets. Whether that is motivated by religion, business, or self-determination is irrelevant. The consciousness to learn from your mistakes is wisdom, and the ability to say, "I'm sorry, I made a mistake," is soul-cleansing.

Leaving opportunities unexplored is like avoiding learning–on purpose. Not making an effort for fear of failure is assuredly giving credence to False Evidence Appearing Real (F.E.A.R.). For me, avoiding failure or judgement is not a strong enough obstacle to make me shy away from what "could" be if only I made an effort. At some point along the way, I realized that my desire for success had to be stronger than my fear of failure.

In my humble opinion, Hell, is the person that I am today running into the person that I could have been if I had only taken more risks, if I had only believed in something or someone other than myself or what I thought, if I had only made an effort.

I don't want to look back and experience regret for being afraid to explore new things, implement new information or strategies, for being afraid of what my friends or family might think of me. Those who love me deserve better than that from me. They deserve the best version of me.

I believe everyone's successes in life spill over to the lives of their loved ones and all those in their space. As we move forward in life, we accumulate more knowledge and resources that will benefit us and those close to us. As we succeed in life, we become a resource for others in our space.

I hope this book will plant seeds for all who read it and foster a desire for their next steps, whatever those steps may be. I pray those who read this book are spurred on to do great things with their life. I genuinely care if this book is a benefit to you personally. I hope it is so impactful that you pass it on so others will also benefit from it.

Thank you, and may you find your Riches Within Reach as you explore A Retirement Cure.

"If you are reading this book,
you will have the opportunity
to change your stars!"

We all have greatness within us. This book will show you how to tap into the riches already within you and suggest that you convert that to an ongoing income–in perpetuity. There's a ton of information being revealed in this book, everything from who we are to who we can be, with some effort.

This technological age we live in allows you—YES, YOU—to create an absolute financial whirlwind for yourself and your family. You simply have to tap into what's already there inside you, build it, sharpen it, polish it, and then unleash it. Your personal income will always be commensurate with your personal development.

I have witnessed or participated in hundreds of thousands of life conversations, and one thing is constant among many people: a serious concern for how to afford to live a comfortable life and enjoy a financially stable retirement.

It's not about retirement; then again, it's **ALL** about retirement. This book is an attempt to encourage you and equip you to create residual income by opening your mind to growth and personal development, if you will.

The ultimate goal is to help provide enough verifiable information and proven methods for those who desire it to realize that it's all about trading Linear Income for Passive Income and Residual Income. The most common way is to let your Linear Income fund the creation of your Passive and Residual Incomes. These different types of incomes will be explored later in this book.

In other words, after reading this book and implementing its ideas, you will have the competence and confidence to utilize your new personal growth to opt out of the status quo concept of retirement and achieve financial independence sooner rather than later. Remember, age does not determine retirement; financial solidity does.

Before we get started, let me ask you a question that I learned from a former manager of mine, Lee. He would ask clients, "Would you spend a dollar to make a dime?"

If your answer is yes, then keep reading; you won't be disappointed.

If you said no, that's awesome too. By the end, you will change your thinking—or won't. Either way, you will gain valuable information to help you along life's journey, so keep reading. However, for grins and giggles, we will revisit that question again in the end.

Young people, listen up! Older people, pay attention! Would you rather work hard for 40 and 50 years to be retired for only 20 years or work hard for just 20 years and be retired for 40 to 50 years? If you are interested in the latter, regardless of age, then read on. Again, you will not be disappointed.

Although it may seem like sometimes, money isn't the focus. Money is just a tool to acquire what you want and, more importantly, provide you with choices. Money is just what we call it today. Yesterday, we were barter–trading cows for horses and pigs for chickens. Tomorrow, we may be trading cryptocurrencies in a paperless digital economy. Today, we have the choice of different types of income.

Oh! Make no mistake; creating these incomes doesn't take that long. As a matter of fact, one concept revealed in this book will increase your financial bottom line immediately this year, the year you are currently living in And it's 99.99% guaranteed if you reside in the United States! So, it really doesn't matter how old you are or how much money you currently have. If you are reading this book, you will have the opportunity to change your stars!

This author believes we should start the conversation with the end in mind. Why? Because the end is the goal. Retirement is the culmination of all the actions and inactions of one's life. Being able to stop working, or what they call retirement, should happen when we are young enough and able enough to enjoy it. Wouldn't you agree?

We should be physically able to check off the items on our bucket list. We should be able to spend time with our friends, children, and grandchildren. If we can just start young enough, we can achieve rather than imagine being retired at 55, 45, 35, or even 25 years old.

Imagine establishing the family legacy that allows your children or grandchildren to be born "retired," as they will never know what it is to work a traditional job. Retirement is the goal, so let's start there and kind of work our way backward.

"Living the lifestyle that one desires without
having to punch a clock or have a boss
is retirement from the corporate world."

Okay, let's get into it. You were probably taught that retirement is all about savings; it's not. First things first, let's get rid of the ancient belief that retirement is based on age, for it isn't; Social Security benefits are. Retirement is based on having enough money or residual income that one does not have to work a traditional job yet still sustain a healthy lifestyle.

Age has zero to do with it, technically. We have all heard of 20- and 30-year-old millionaires who don't have a job. The Internet has changed things. Social media platforms have given younger people avenues to make significant income. Wise investing, crowdfunding, network and affiliate marketing, and even cryptocurrencies have changed the playing field. Living the lifestyle that one desires without having to punch a clock or have a boss *is retirement* from the corporate world.

Traditionally, we're taught that if you properly prepare for retirement, then you can live out your "golden years" in relative comfort. If you continue to read on, then you will learn, if you don't already know, that retirement, as sold to the masses today, is a concept that used to work but does not work any longer. Traditional retirement is a dying concept. Let's explore.

People looking at retirement usually find that they do not have enough savings to afford higher prices yearly nor enough assets to fall back on. They also discover they do not have access to affordable healthcare in retirement. Therefore, many people reach the government-assigned age for retirement just to find out they must keep working to survive.

Challenges such as ever-increasing taxes and inflation, 401K's and pensions disappearing, rising costs of healthcare, reductions in coverage benefits, and previous medical tax deductions being eliminated are all being suffered by the vast majority of those who followed the traditional retirement blueprint. If someone researches the retirement landscape today, they will find some disturbing statistics.

Studies show outliving their savings is what 60% of older Americans fear most. Also, 59% of retirees rely heavily on Social Security benefits. This is a horrible situation to be in, as the average Social Security check for a retired worker is about $1,360 per month, which is an insult after contributing to this fund for over 40 years.

If that wasn't bad enough, realize that over 40% of single seniors 65 and older get at least 90% of their income from Social Security. Add this to the fact that 44% of retirees carry a crippling amount of debt, and it's easy to see retirement doesn't provide enough funds to live, only to survive.

Did you know studies show that 45% of retirees have no retirement savings AT ALL WHATSOEVER? That tracks as true because studies show that only half of Americans feel they have saved enough for retirement, and as such, 30% of Retirees have postponed their Retirement plans. As a matter of fact, 30% of Retirees stop contributing to their Retirement accounts altogether. Actually, more than one-third of Americans expect to work in Retirement, and only 25% of people say they don't plan to work.

Healthcare costs continue to grow faster than wages and returns on investments. For example, a Retired couple can expect to spend about $260,000 during Retirement on healthcare alone. During my research, I found that most people believe their cost of living is higher now than it will be in Retirement. However, studies show that almost half of Retirement households spend more money, not less, during Retirement.

The average baby boomer has $163,577 saved for Retirement; over a 15-year Retirement span, that's only about $908 per month—tragic. This information is beginning to become common knowledge, and now, almost 25% of current workers expect to retire at age 70 or even older.

Hence, many Retirees are going back to school so they can earn a higher wage, which is awesome. However, just $30,000 in student loan debt can mean $325,000 less in retirement savings. Many need the additional income because studies show that 30% of homeowners aged 65 and older still have a mortgage payment.

In addition to all of these disturbing study results, one out of every four people who are 65 or older today will live past age 90, and one in ten will live past age 95. Thinking about their financial predicament is depressing.

Unfortunately, that's not all. The most disturbing fact these studies revealed was that seniors are America's fastest-growing group of bankruptcy filers. After working and contributing for 40-plus years, the end of the road is to NOT have enough money to survive and then go through the process of admitted failure of filing bankruptcy. To me, that's just heart-wrenching.

Retirement should be about relaxing and enjoying family. Retirement should be our fondest years. Retirement is hard-earned and well-deserved **ME** time, time to enjoy everything previously sacrificed. What Retirement should **NOT** be is stressing, worrying, struggling, continued sacrificing, and disappointing. I'm sure you would agree. However, each generation has its own Retirement thoughts and expectations, and studies show those expectations are not very desirable.

"Now, the market they're driving is the Retirement Market,

otherwise known as the Social Security and Medicare Funds."

There are six generations associated with the 20th Century. Arguably, their approximate dates and titles are as follows: The Greatest Generation (GI Generation) - 1901–1924; The Silent Generation - 1928–1945; The Baby Boom Generation - 1946–1964; Generation X - 1965–1980; Millennial Generation or Generation Y - 1981–1996; and Generation Z or iGen - 1997–2010. Each has its own social and economic challenges.

The Center for Generational Kinetics recognizes the last five generations and has provided studies and statistics. There is good and bad news for each generation. Let's take a very brief look at that landscape.

The Greatest Generation: People born between 1901 and 1924 are the first of the 20th century. They endured a changing America and set the foundation for what we see today. They are at least 98 years old and have passed or are passing what wealth they have accumulated down through their families.

The Silent Generation: People born between 1928 and 1945 have done their part in society. This is when Retirement worked as designed. They went to school, got good grades, developed a career, and retired with the gold watch. At the end of this generation, America went to war. The soldiers came home and created babies at an unprecedented rate, which gave birth to the baby boomers.

"Almost exactly nine months after World War II ended, the cry of the baby was heard across the land," as historian Landon Jones later described the trend. "More babies were born in 1946 than ever before: 3.4 million, 20 percent more than in 1945. This was the beginning of the so-called "baby boom." In 1947, another 3.8 million babies were born; 3.9 million were born in 1952; and more than 4 million were born yearly from 1954 until 1964, when the boom finally tapered off. By then, there were 76.4 million "baby boomers" in the United States. They made up almost 40 percent of the nation's population."[1]

The baby boomers, born between 1946 and 1964, were the largest generation in the history of the world until the millennial generation and have been the target of most businesses throughout their timeline. The baby boomers created new business markets and exploded other markets simply because, "As the largest generational group in U.S. history (until the millennial generation slightly surpassed them), baby boomers have had—and continue to have—a significant impact on the economy. As a result, they are often the focus of marketing campaigns and business plans."[2]

For example, as children, the Baby Boomers gave birth to the coonskin cap surge of the 1950s. Disney's Davy Crockett sensation created sales of over $300 million in the mid-50s ($2.6 Billion in 2014 dollars).[3] Toys like the teddy bear, frisbee, yo-yo, and Ouija board created a large economic segment in the boomers' toy market.

One study said it best when it stated, "As the wealthiest social cohort, baby boomers influence key purchasing decisions. In the United States alone, boomers held nearly $59 trillion in household wealth in 2020. Their wealth doubles that of Gen X and outnumbers that of millennials, who are just entering the prime of adulthood. This generational patterned distribution of wealth is also seen in Europe and Asia, which means that the boomers have a global capacity for driving major trends in consuming, spending, and funding."[4]

Aging boomers drove and continue to drive multiple markets. Now, the market they're driving is the Retirement Market, otherwise known as the Social Security and Medicare Funds. Sadly, the vast majority of boomers are finding out they are not as financially stable and have to change their retirement plans and dreams.

If I told you we are all working hard for a 5% chance to have a successful life, would you be okay with those odds? Let me put it this way: if you and 99 other people went up in an airplane and were going to jump out with a parachute, and the instructor told everyone that only 5% of the parachutes were going to open, would you still jump?

Well, in the real world, you've already jumped financially. Let me explain. We work hard for most of our lives, make sacrifices, save as best we can, and invest wisely, and statistics show that only 5% of us will be able to retire successfully. In other words, you've already jumped, but it takes 40 years to hit the ground or realize that you have a parachute that isn't going to open.

That's the old-fashioned 40/40/40 Plan we have all been taught for generations. We'll dive into its solution later. It's called the 10-4 Marketing Plan, and it will challenge what you have been conditioned to believe.

Oh, remember "Savings?" Do you realize that you would have to have about one million dollars saved when you retire just to have five thousand per month to survive?

This is why many seniors still work, survive on a strict budget, depend on the government, or, unfortunately, live in deplorable conditions. Successful retirement in today's economy using this outdated thought process is a proven recipe for disaster and disappointment.

If we had only been conditioned and programmed from the time of birth to focus on retirement, just as fervently as we were conditioned to believe in Santa, the Easter Bunny, and the Tooth Fairy, retirement would still be a wonderful and satisfying realization of reaping from a lifetime of sowing.

Since this is unimaginably important, and I feel like some of you may have missed this critical point, I'm going to say it again differently.

What if we had been programmed, from the beginning, to understand the use of the living benefits of life insurance? Can you imagine the wealth and legacy one could create if they had only set themselves and their children up properly with their life insurance beginning on the day of birth?

The income created from the living benefits is the same income that can be invested wisely, creating multiple income streams. Properly done, generational wealth would be inevitable. By the way, it's not too late.

"The internet connects the entire world, and what used to take weeks now takes hours or even minutes."

Think about this, please. In a nutshell, we are conditioned to believe that if we just work hard, sacrifice, only spend money on necessities, and save and invest our money, we will eventually live a successful retirement. However, the unspoken challenge is that our world has changed; business and money move faster than ever before.

For example, the invention of the fax machine increased the speed at which we do business. The beeper or pager increased the pace even further. Cell phones changed communication forever and, in doing so, increased the speed of business decisions, which in turn further increased the speed and frequency of transactions and sales. We must also consider the incredible increase in the speed of commerce using Blockchain, with the new digital currencies replacing fiat dollars and coins.

The internet connects the entire world. What used to take weeks now takes hours or even minutes. If business can move this quickly and money exchanges hands so much faster, then why does our personal income grow so slowly?

Why are we willing to believe if we go into debt, spending tens of thousands of dollars for four years of college, that we will be successful in life when the statistics show that just a tiny percentage of people retire successfully?

Why do we keep believing in the insanity of doing the same thing and expect different results? Are we going to more advanced schools? Are we learning a different curriculum with personal development at its core? Are we living a better lifestyle in today's economy with the resulting jobs? Why do we continue to accept the programming of traditional beliefs and wholeheartedly believe we will achieve different results in this new world?

Studies show that our income cannot keep up with taxes and inflation and never has. As previously stated, the 40/40/40 Plan is to work 40 hours per week for 40 years just to survive on 40 percent of what we've earned. This may have worked decades ago, but it is no longer a viable plan. So, why do we continue to do what doesn't work anymore?

I know it's hard to believe and even more difficult to accept as there are many factors involved with retirement, such as age, health, financial stability, savings, investments, inflation, and economic times (the cost of milk, cheese, bread, etc., in the future), so here are some facts to consider.

- Starting with the COVID-19 Pandemic – "...40% of Americans are afraid they won't be able to retire because of financial setbacks related to the pandemic."

- "Retirement savings for households in the bottom 25% of net worth grew by $2,710 from 1989 to 2019. Savings for the top 10% of net worth grew by over $600,000 during that same time period."[5]

- "Of the 47.8 million Americans ages 65 and older, the average income is only $38,515, according to the U.S. Census, and their average net worth is $170,516. With numbers like that, saving for retirement can be challenging."[6]

- "Collectively, health problems, caring for family, and lack of work contributed to the timing of retirement for 45 percent of retirees."[7]

- "Many Americans are in a difficult financial situation with only about $17,500 in retirement savings for those between the age of 56 and 61."[8]

- "The proverbial three-legged retirement stool is shakier than ever. Social Security and Medicare face financing shortfalls, while pension plans have largely disappeared for younger workers."[9]

- "Half of U.S. households will not have enough retirement income to maintain their pre-retirement standard of living, according to the Center for Retirement Research at Boston College."[9]

- "Social Security only has enough funds to pay full benefits until 2033, and Medicare is projected to be depleted in 2026."[9]

- "Meanwhile, more than 44 million people owe a collective $1.7 trillion in student loan debt, according to Bankrate, and 51% of Americans have less than three months' worth of emergency savings."[9]

According to these nine statistics, it is overwhelmingly evident that retirement instruments and the financial planning methods of the past have not and will not work for the vast majority of people moving forward. "If people aren't able to withstand a crisis like the pandemic or another emergency, how are people actually going to be able to retire with dignity or retire at all?" said Alejandra Montoya-Boyer, director of policy at Prosperity Now.[9] Those who choose to rely on outdated financial instruments and antiquated retirement advice will follow in the disappointed footsteps of the tens of millions of people who came before them.

That said, there is a solution. There are new rules and new advice. If you are not already familiar with Robert Kiyosaki, his new rules of money have proven to be correct. His Rich Dad Poor Dad series has proven to advise and educate us on how to change our thinking and improve our chances of living the lifestyle we desire now and retiring successfully.

It's called the 10-4 Marketing Plan and ends with you having the ability to live out your goals and dreams, unlike the current 40/40/40 Plan society offers. The 10-4 Marketing Plan is rooted in entrepreneurship.

It requires you to think differently than you have before so you can do things differently than you have in the past.

"Unlike money, when we spend time,

it's just gone, forever."

The first step is deciding WHY you want financial success. That WHY has to be so deep, defined, and desirable to you that you will want to succeed more than anything. Do you want your WHY so bad that you will do whatever it takes, just like the five percenters?

This is where the rubber meets the road. This is what must happen: a decision has to be made. Your WHY has to make you cry. Your WANT to succeed has to become a NEED to succeed. A belief has to become an action. That action has to be based on solid, useful information.

As Eric Thomas said, "When you WANT success as bad as you NEED to breathe, then and only then will you have success." Until then, you will not have the commitment and determination necessary to do whatever it takes to ensure your success, which, of course, has to be legal, moral, and ethical.

Most people fool themselves into thinking they are doing what they need to do but are really doing what they want to do. We must guard ourselves when it comes to wasting time and money. The acronym is called SYSTEM: Save Yourself Some Time Energy Money.

Time is one of our most valuable commodities. Unlike money, when we spend time, it's just gone forever. We can always make more money, but we cannot make more time. We have to spend our time wisely. We have to ensure we are spending our time in the most productive manner possible to maximize results.

For example, for networkers, we need to spend our time doing the Daily Business Building Activities (D.B.B.A.). In our everyday lives, we need to ensure we spend our most valuable time doing the things that bring us the most positive results. First, we need to be familiar with the 80/20 rule.

"The 80-20 rule, also known as the Pareto Principle, is a familiar saying that asserts that 80% of outcomes (or outputs) result from 20% of all causes (or inputs) for any given event. Although the 80-20 Rule is frequently used in business and economics, you can apply the concept to any field, wealth distribution, personal finance, and spending habits."[10]

Otherwise stated, "The Pareto Principle states that for many outcomes, roughly 80% of consequences come from 20% of causes. In other words, a small percentage of causes have an outsized effect. This concept is important to understand because it can help you identify which initiatives to prioritize so you can make the most impact."[11]

"So, what, 20% of your work drives 80% of your outcomes? No matter what your situation, it's important to remember that there are only so many minutes in an hour, hours in a day, and days in a week.

Pareto can help you to see this is a good thing; otherwise, you'd be a slave to a never-ending list of things to do."[12]

"Where does the Pareto Principle come from?" The Pareto Principle was developed by Italian economist Vilfredo Pareto in 1896. Pareto observed that 80% of the land in Italy was owned by only 20% of the population. He also witnessed this happening with plants in his garden—20% of his plants were bearing 80% of the fruit.

This relationship is best mathematically described as a power law distribution between two quantities, in which a change in one quantity results in a relevant change in the other. The 80/20 rule is not a formal mathematical equation but more a generalized phenomenon that can be observed in economics, business, time management, and even sports.

- 20% of a plant contains 80% of the fruit

- 80% of a company's profit comes from 20% of customers

- 20% of players result in 80% of points scored

- The basis of the Pareto Principle states that 80% of results come from 20% of actions

"While it doesn't always come to be an exact 80/20 ratio, this imbalance is often seen in various business cases:

- 20% of the sales reps generate 80% of total sales

- 20% of customers account for 80% of total profits

- 20% of the most reported software bugs cause 80% of software crashes

- 20% of patients account for 80% of healthcare spending"[12]

As you can see, if we focus 80% of our efforts on the 20% of activities that yield the best and most profitable results, we can succeed faster than we ever have before.

For example, let's say you are good at closing sales but not at cold calling. Rather than attempting to get better at cold calling, find a team member who is good at cold calling, team up, and let them cold call for you both, and you close sales for you both.

Another alternative is to outsource what you are not good at so you can focus on your areas of strength. They say teamwork makes the dream work, but they also say if you want something done right, you have to do it yourself. These types of programming contradictions keep us from capitalizing on our strengths and minimizing our weaknesses. We all need to stay disciplined and focused on our WHY so we can achieve on unprecedented levels.

Darren Hardy of Success Magazine inspired this training many years ago. He made me think; maybe it's time to *Pick A Fight!* When cornered, we have a natural built-in instinct known as Fight or Flight. Life brings challenges. Life happens. It's natural to deal with life's challenges in a way that avoids pain. The majority of experts in the psychology field will tell you that we, as humans, will make decisions that help us avoid feeling pain.

We stay in an undesirable marriage rather than face ridicule from family and friends. We endure an unhealthy relationship to avoid admitting we had a failed marriage. We stay even though every fiber of our being tells us to end it so we don't have to face judgment from those around us. We'll settle for an abusive relationship because being alone feels worse. Why? Because, for many of us, we'd rather stay and deal with it than deal with the fallout, the pain.

Why do we stay in dead-end jobs? In those situations, we know there is no growth opportunity with that company. Many remain in a hostile work environment. Some deal with sexual harassment regularly but won't quit that job. We know we are underpaid and overworked, but we tell ourselves that all jobs are the same or that we can't find a better job and won't make as much elsewhere. The job is closer to our home. We give ourselves any number of excuses to ensure we avoid pain.

Sometimes, we just need to Pick A Fight. Having an enemy makes us step up and take massive action. An enemy can provide purpose, motivation, and encouragement. Almost everything has a natural enemy. Light has Dark. Good has Evil. Right has Wrong. Freedom has Restrictions. Positive has Negative. Income has Debt. Residual Income has Linear Income. Wealth has Poverty. Hand-ups have Handouts. Microsoft has Apple. FedEx has UPS. Dreamers have Skeptics.

Batman has the Joker. Luke Skywalker has Darth Vader. David had Goliath. Rocky had Apollo. I'm sure you get the drift.

An enemy gives us a reason to fight. Having to fight challenges our skills, character, purpose, and resolve. Having to fight forces us to assess and exercise our talents and abilities. When we choose to fight instead of take flight, we are forced to step up to the plate and swing the bat. That attempt alone gives us a chance to succeed, excel, and achieve. Without a fight, we can become comfortable, lazy, and sedentary, mentally. We can lose our purpose, passion, and vigor.

If you want to identify your enemy, simply decide what you really want in life; determine your WHY. Write down that WHY, your dreams, and your goals. Then, identify the opposite of those. Make a list of those opposites, the things holding you back from achieving or obtaining that WHY. They are the enemies.

Put them on the wall and throw darts at them. Determine what you need to do to overcome those obstacles. Get the tools, training, or resources needed to overcome those challenges without delay. Only action conquers fear. Write the steps down, date them, and begin to move deliberately. Make necessary adjustments along the way.

Do you want to get excited? Do you want to rally troops? Do you want to ignite a team? Do you want to get people all fired up? Then find an enemy and Pick A Fight!

Doing this on our own limits us to our own abilities. We can only go as far as our own resources, connections, knowledge, and ambition will take us. We set ourselves up for failure which is why most of us have trouble achieving our goals and dreams. It's not possible for us to be good at everything.

We all have talents, but no one is talented in every aspect needed for success in any field. We may be great at art, science, hair styling, or mathematics. Still, we may need someone to help us with things we are not good with, such as editing, marketing and advertising, SEO, or even negotiating a fair and equitable contract.

Many times, I have shared a story titled "Everybody, Somebody, Anybody, and Nobody," but with a little twist. The lesson of the story is clear: "… no one took responsibility, so nothing got accomplished. It's a story that plays out often in organizations and companies and on teams—anywhere there is culture that lacks accountability…"[13] However, this story can have a very deep impact on your life if you read it carefully by simply adding the word "ELSE." It goes as follows.

This is a story about "Somebody Else." There was something important to be done, and Everybody was asked to do it. Everybody knew *Somebody Else* would do it. Although Anybody could have done it, Nobody wanted to do it. *Somebody Else* got angry because it was Everybody's responsibility to do it. Nobody realized that Everybody wouldn't do it and expected *Somebody Else* to do it. Well, Everybody blamed *Somebody Else*, so of course, and as usual, *Somebody Else* ended up doing it. *Somebody Else* is the one who gets things done, which is why *Somebody Else* is so experienced, talented, and successful. Doesn't it make sense to have *Somebody Else* in your corner or on your team?

I cannot remember what book I read it in so I can give them their credit (possibly The Slight Edge by Jeff Olson), but I'll never forget the quote, "99% of everything we ever wanted to obtain or achieve, requires the cooperation of Someone Else."

To achieve our own dreams and goals, we need *Somebody Else* to have dreams and goals, and, in their success, we have the tools we need for our own success. If *Somebody Else* didn't have the dream of creating the old-fashioned typewriter, I wouldn't be typing this sentence on this laptop.

In my training classes, I used to ask the attendees a series of questions, and the answer was always the same. So, ask yourself, who is driving your dream car? *Somebody Else*. Who is living in your dream home? *Somebody Else*. Who is the richest person in the world? *Somebody Else*. Who is the nicest, prettiest, smartest, most courageous, most thoughtful person in the world? *Somebody Else* was always the answer. Regardless of how good you are, we all need *Somebody Else* on our team to help us be our best. That's why a team will always have more success than any individual. Ask Michael Jordan.

"Teams are successful because they combine their strengths,
eliminating their individual weaknesses."

Much of what we do is done using the Internet, so you can easily collaborate with *Somebody Else*, partake in all the trainings and information required, and tap into the resources necessary to elevate your game.

Teams are successful because they combine their strengths, eliminating their individual weaknesses, which allows *Somebody Else* to help each other grow faster. Anyone serious about achieving their goals must have a hunger for success and be able to follow *Somebody Else's* instructions and advice, and then they can succeed with a team backing them. You can be *"Somebody Else"* for *"Somebody Else."*

This author believes working together is the answer. You have tried it on your own; now try working with *Somebody Else*, and a team can help you have more success than you have ever had before. Let *Somebody Else* help you brighten your life and unleash your potential by showing you how to obtain your dreams, goals, and desires.

You do the easy part, the part you're good at, and let *Somebody Else* do the heavy lifting for you and with you. *Somebody Else* has made the websites and presentation videos. *Somebody Else* has created the training videos. They are on YouTube already.

Somebody Else has the expertise, intelligence, and skills to help you get where you want to go. Leverage the resources that *Somebody Else* brings to the table so you both can mutually benefit from the partnership.

Doesn't it just make sense to partner with *Somebody Else* who has strengths in the areas you are weak, who has assets you don't have, who has knowledge you haven't been exposed to, and who has information you don't know?

No one knows everything. I certainly don't. I believe there is more that I don't know than there is that I do know. I have had people teach me all my life, from grade school to my first job to my career in sales and networking. All of that time, I have had people around me to train me and show me how to do my job, to do things correctly and successfully.

I have been blessed to build very large teams and have incredible success in network and affiliate marketing as well as a very successful sales career. I had been a leader in my field for years when Raza, a colleague in Toronto, Canada, said something to me that inspired a training very similar to what he was doing.

In that training, my beginning question was, what determines what we have in life? More accurately, what determines what we have and don't have?

"It wasn't a question of right and wrong.
It was a question of how and what people thought."

For each individual, what is it that creates our individual situations throughout our lives? What really creates our Haves and Don't Haves? We all have wants and needs. We all have responsibilities to ourselves and our loved ones.

What determines how we handle those situations? What determines what resources we have at our disposal at that moment? *I submit how and what we do determine what we have and don't have in life.*

How and what we do are DECISIONS we have made or didn't make. We decide to do something or decide not to do something. We decide to say something or decide not to say something. Our decisions in life, in other words, what we do and don't do, determine what we have and don't have. Would you agree?

Most of us have said if we could go back in time and make a different decision—handle a situation differently—we would. Since hindsight is 20/20, I'm sure we all have one or more situations we would have handled differently back then, knowing what we know now. So, the question becomes, what determines what we do and don't do? *I submit how and what we think determines what we do and don't do.*

How and what we think guides our decisions. How we think and what we think make up our decision-making process. One controversial topic I used in my training was politics because I was guaranteed to get different viewpoints. I knew half the attendees would feel one way, and the other half would feel the opposite way. It wasn't a question of right and wrong. It was a question of how and what people thought.

I know humans are creatures of habit and comfort. So, I would introduce a second topic—theft. Only those who felt strongly would speak out and say anything at all. Most people would only share their answers by facial expression.

To explore how people think differently, I asked the group if a mother of three children were starving and the mother stole food from a grocery store, should she be convicted as a common thief?

But here's a twist: she didn't steal any food for herself, only for the three children. Invariably, I would have opposing viewpoints. Why? Because *I submit that how and what we think is determined by what we believe.*

How we were raised and what we believe determines our moral base. What we believe allows us to feel convicted in our reasoning. Often, we justify our actions, but we don't have to justify our beliefs. A belief can't be right or wrong; it's just a belief.

Many of us get our belief structure from our parents or guardians. Others build their belief structure on religion. Others use a mix of rearing and religion. As we mature in life, we develop our own modified belief structure.

Most humans are born with the ability to know when we are doing right and wrong, but some of us will rationalize right and wrong with justifiable reasons, which will be based on what we believe.

HAVE ← DO ← THINK ← BELIEVE

Our *Beliefs* determines how we *Think/Don't Think,* which determines what we *Do/Don't Do,* which determines what we *Have/Don't Have.* So many of us are conditioned or programmed to believe the path to fixing issues in our lives is to change what we do and don't do.

Go back to school, move to another city or state, date a different person, or change jobs. This type of fix is a band-aid. This thought process will not change the behavior. It will only change the buildings and faces around you because no matter where **YOU** go, there **YOU** are.

You will still value the same types of things, attract the same caliber of people, and make the same decisions that got you in that situation somewhere else. The solution isn't in the *Do* stage; the answer resides in the *Believe* stage.

The same brain will yield the same thought process. You need a different thought process to yield different results. You have to *BELIEVE* differently so you can *THINK* differently to *DO* things differently and *HAVE* different results.

I previously referenced Robert Kiyosaki. His resume is above reproach. He introduced us to the new rules of money through his Rich Dad Poor Dad series. In a nutshell, he says that the old rules of money and creating wealth are obsolete. He proves the old ways of thinking about money, making money, and saving money do not work in today's economy.

His Cashflow Quadrant explains there are four ways to make money. We'll dive deeper into those four quadrants later. For now, since money is a common denominator, let's look at it more closely.

We can all use more money. Do we have to have more money? Probably not. I'm sure we can make some changes and sacrifices to ensure we survive. However, I believe we can all use more money, even if we spend it all in charitable ways.

Maybe you don't need more money, but I'm willing to wager that you know people that you would help even more than you already do if you had more money. Okay, now that we have rid ourselves of any self-righteousness, let's explore making more money. We'll start with a few questions.

How are you "spending" your time? Remember, unlike money, time spent is gone forever. Are you being paid what you're worth? Do you live the lifestyle that you desire? Are you working for your dreams and goals or the dreams and goals of your company owner? Do you believe you can retire at the age and comfort level you worked hard for? Okay, here are some statistical facts and more thought-provoking questions.

"We have 8 hours per day to live our best life."

99% of people today ARE the company workforce (people who actually have a job). CEOs and high-paid people comprise only about 1% of the labor force.

99% of people today need a raise but do not have the time necessary to make it happen with another job. Are you the 1%, or do you need a raise?

Time is money, right? How does the average person spend their 24 hours per day, or, better yet, how do *you* "spend" *your* 24 hours each day?

Let's look at what I call the "Time Pie."

The traditional and ideal breakdown has several factors; however, we will keep it simple. Here we go. Doctors recommend we spend 8 hours Sleeping. Society or social norms dictate that we spend 8 hours

Working, which leaves us just 8 hours to Live our lives. Did you get that? We have 8 hours per day to live our best life.

Life has its own challenges, but let's just stick to the basics. Living life includes spending time with family and loved ones, showers, relaxing with a book or the Internet, watching a little television to keep up with current events, fellowship, shopping for groceries, cooking, eating right, exercising, cleaning up after each meal, cleaning the rest of the home, doing laundry, running errands, paying bills, yard work, home maintenance, car maintenance, children's extra-curricular activities, PTA meetings or helping with homework, doctor and dentist visits for the family, and your daily commute, just to name a few.

Curveball!

What do you do when life happens, you know, when you need more money? For example, the car breaks down, a child becomes ill, or you get sick.

Most cut into their 8 hours of sleeping or sacrifice several items from their living life list because they must work. Sometimes, people have to work voluntary overtime, get a second job, work on holidays, or are even subjected to mandatory overtime. We need more money, right?

So, we're in the designed trap of trading more hours for dollars. Hours we must take from somewhere else, from another part of the Time Pie.

As I mentioned, we take from the sleeping category, making us less alert and less sharp. We miss things because we're mentally slower. We're groggier and more short-tempered, which can cause a host of other problems.

We also take from our living life category and fail to do things we need to do. We spend less time with that sick friend or relative. We miss our children's after-school activities. We simply don't "have time" to do all the things we need to do to have a comfortable life. We sacrifice— because that's what we were taught to believe.

Life spills over into both the sleeping and living life categories even further, does it not? Then, the domino effect kicks in, and the body breaks down. The mind begins to break down. We don't eat right. We don't sleep right. We begin to stress over things we need to do but don't "have time" for. We miss days at work, which is losing money for most of us. We have doctor visits and have to buy prescriptions, costing us even more money. The cycle continues with no end in sight.

We still hold out hope that something will give, and we'll catch a break. We'll catch up on the credit card bill when we get that raise or promotion. Some of us think a second job will solve this dilemma. We just have to continue to give up on sleeping and living an enjoyable life. "It's only for a short time." "I'll be alright." "I have to put in the work." "It has to end at some point, right?" Sound familiar?

Here's a question for you: If you continue doing the same thing repeatedly, what makes you think you'll achieve different results? It is the opinion of this author that you have to begin to change what you believe so you can change how you think, which will change what you do so you can have something different.

Well, how bad do you want that change? Are you willing to explore a new train of thought? If so, you may just be able to break free of the status quo and become one of the one-percenters. For those who don't know, only 1% of Americans make at least $250,000 a year. Personally, I think that's a tragic statistic for "the greatest country in the world."

One of my most in-depth training is called "Know Who You're Talking To." It is a culmination of years of research and decades of experience. The information is derived from:

- 'I Must' by Kim Kiyosaki
- The Meyers-Briggs System
- The Merrill-Wilson System
- Personality Plus by Florence Littauer
- Power Persuasion by Barron & Kaus
- Cashflow Quadrant by Robert Kiyosaki
- The Science of Influence by Kevin Hogan
- 21 Irrefutable Laws of Leadership by John C Maxwell
- Decades of mentorship by successful Entrepreneurs such as Bill & Peggy Britt, John and Jennie Bell Crowe, Sheldon and Marilee Layman, and Dr. John C. Maxwell

- The training titled Believe, Learn, Practice, & Teach by Kenneth & Lisa Bristol
- Dozens of instructional workbooks
- Hundreds of hours of reading self-help and leadership material
- Thousands of hours of listening to self-help and leadership material
- University studies on Applied Behavioral Sciences
- Thirty years of experience in Sales
- Literally, decades of irritating people because of me using them for practice

These books, classes, seminars, interviews, mentorship sessions, websites, as well as my personal interactions with thousands of people from all walks of life, have shared enough information to know how people act and react, what people value, and how they process information. As they say, "There is nothing new under the sun." People are predictable to a degree. Yes, everyone is different, but we all have common traits that can be quantified and influenced.

"That one piece of information

is what drives their motivations."

In the spirit of learning and doing things differently, let's start with learning people. People often say, "It's not what you say; it's how you say it." I believe "Knowing Who You're Talking To" is just as important.

Let's face it: it's tough to sell glasses to someone with 20/20 vision. It's equally as difficult to motivate people to do what they need to do or do what you need them to do. For example, why do so many parents have such a hard time getting children to clean their bedrooms, wash the dishes, or take out the trash without a fight?

We have to learn to invest in people, including ourselves, so take the time to ask questions. Sincerely care about them enough to probe deeper to find out their motivations and triggers. For people in sales or those whose daily activities require influence (moms and dads), this is where you **Probe**, **Qualify**, and **Pre-Qualify**. Care enough to find out their WHY. That one piece of information is what drives their motivations.

I take it a step further and find the "WHY behind the WHY." That information is critical if you want to "move" them. You absolutely must spend the time getting to know them on a deeper level. How quickly you can do this depends on your ability to build rapport. We'll get into depth about that shortly.

A quick word on our WHY. I mentioned it before when referring to picking a fight and identifying an enemy. I'm revisiting the topic because it is one of the most important pieces of the puzzle. You have to care enough about yourself and others to identify the WHY. Why people will do something is the very information you need to make them happy and to make yourself happy.

Our WHY is our motivation. Our WHY is our reasoning. Our WHY will make us do that thing we have been avoiding. Our WHY is our justification for something we did or said. Our WHY will make us change our behavior. Knowing the WHY is crucial. To take it deeper, the WHY behind the WHY is what I refer to as OUR TRUTH. Let me explain.

We all lie to ourselves, whether we know it or believe it or not. I know I lie to myself daily. I give myself awesome reasons I should or should not do or have done something. I give myself great-sounding reasons for saying something I shouldn't have said. My father used to say, "The more intelligent you are, the more intelligent excuses you give yourself."

We all justify our WHY all the time. However, the WHY behind the WHY is our truth. Allow me to demonstrate. Why did we give that homeless person (cousin, brother, sister, or friend) money? Because they needed it or because they asked for it. Truth: Because we wanted to.

But WHY did we want to? Because they needed it or because they wanted it. Deep Truth: Because it made us feel better that we did it. WHY did it feel good to do it? Because we could help someone in need. Deeper Truth: Because doing something that makes me feel good raises my self-esteem. WHY do we need to raise our self-esteem? Even Deeper Truth: Because we're damaged or have been in a similar situation.

I could keep going deeper, but I hope you get the point. The reason we were willing to give the money wasn't because they needed it or wanted it. That was a lie we told ourselves. It wasn't because it made us feel good, which was only a side effect. It wasn't because it raised our self-esteem, which was a result. All of these are justifications we tell ourselves. Little tiny lies.

We gave the money because, for one reason or another, we sympathized. I could take it even deeper to specific situations and feelings. Again, I hope you get the point of how important the WHY is. If you know someone's WHY, or better yet, their WHY behind the WHY, then you have access to what will motivate them to do or not do something. This will come from knowing who you're talking to. That process involves building rapport.

Building rapport and the Law of Attraction have similar facets but are very different. The age-old principle called the Law of Attraction (LOA) basically states that positive comes from positive and negative comes from negative. Many of us don't realize that our thoughts govern much of our lives. What makes people think that a negative approach to a situation will yield a positive outcome if thoughts are energy?

LOA suggests the thoughts we put into a project will profoundly affect the project results. The reasoning behind it is the belief that thoughts are energy. If thoughts are made up of energy, then positive and negative energy can spill over into every facet of our lives, as that energy is a part of our decision-making process.

Albeit, many aspects of LOA can be interpreted in different ways. For example, many people believe success and failure can be attributed to manifestation. Others believe meditation will bring forth the desired results. Yet, others believe the holy grail is determination, commitment, perseverance, or even timing. Who's right and who's wrong? Who really knows, right?

LOA simply states that like attracts like. We say things like, "You have to give to receive," "What you think about you bring about," and

"Birds of a feather flock together." Sound familiar? All of these are examples of LOA. Simply put, if you think negatively, then negative influences will infiltrate your life, and the same applies to positive thinkers.

Some people believe this universal law is governed by the cosmos or the universe, and still, others believe it is the positive or negative vibrations that we put out into the world that bring us back a positive or negative result/return.

Many self-help gurus and personal development experts make statements that lead one to believe the energy that comes from our thoughts goes out into the world and comes back to us from the world. It's fine for you to believe that because that may be true. Who knows?

I believe the power of manifestation and attraction is based on the gospel. My "belief" is rooted in spirituality. Scripture is clear as it reveals that the created and the creator are not the same. That's like saying man has the same power and energy as the omnipotent being that man calls God, which is not the case.

Scripture refers to LOA directly and indirectly. An example of an indirect reference is Matthew 21:22 (KJV), which states, "Anything that you ask in prayer, believe that it will be given to you." This illustrates that our outcomes are not based on our own power, and we are simply an influence based on belief and obedience.

An example of a direct reference is Proverbs 4:23 (KJV), which states, "Be careful how you think; your life is shaped by your thoughts." Notice the same reference to the importance and power of our thoughts regarding our lives.

Whether you believe in an omnipotent being or believe you have the power, the point remains the same: take care of your thoughts, as they can profoundly impact every aspect of your life.

Okay, back to building rapport. Developing the ability to build rapport can take you to unimaginable heights. Throughout a conversation, people will let you know who they are if you care enough about them to not "hear" them but "listen" to them.

It is infinitely easier to "connect" with people if you know who they are, and connecting is everything. Humans need to know, like, or trust you to move forward with you without regrets, also known as Buyer's Remorse. In sales, we call those be-backs and chargebacks, which no one likes.

"Different personalities have different mindsets and trigger words."

LISTEN to people. Deliver your information in a way that is easy for them to process. Use their exact same wording when you explore deeper with questions. You need to care enough to "LISTEN" to them. It is about them, not you. Most of us cannot resist the urge to insert ourselves into the conversation.

For example, a young lady explained to me that she took care of her mother for the last five years of her mother's life. She described how she had to give up everything to care for her mother day in and day out, 24-hour care. I asked questions about how she cared for her mother, whether she had to bathe her, feed her, and cook for her; questions like that because I cared, and it gave me insight into her WHY.

Another woman walked up and joined the conversation. At her first chance, she began to describe how she had to care for her father under very similar circumstances. To this day, if I call that young lady and ask for a favor, she is very willing to help since she likes me because she feels like I care about her and her family, which I genuinely do. The real reason is that I spent time building rapport with her. I spoke to her in a way that she could resonate with my feelings and thoughts. It made her feel like I was easy to talk to. She now feels like she knows, likes, or trusts me, which is imperative when it comes to believing in someone.

Different personalities process information in different ways. Different personalities have different mindsets and trigger words. For example, people who speak quickly like to process information quickly. If you speak too slowly for someone who processes information quickly, you will lose them along the way. This is not because they do not know, understand, or are not interested in what you're saying; it's only because they cannot "process" what you're saying, simply because you're saying it too slowly for them to process it. You have to know who you're talking to.

Have you ever found yourself repeatedly explaining, re-explaining, and re-wording a question or statement because the other person was not "getting it" or understanding you? Sure, we all have. The reason is that they could not "process" what you were saying. You were not speaking to them in a way they could process the information.

Are you talking to an employee like they're a business owner? Are you talking to a lazy person like they're a go-getter? Are you talking to a selfish person about being part of a team? Are you talking to an unmotivated person about being successful? Are you talking to a know-it-all about learning and following? Are you talking to a loner about participation and contribution? Are you talking to a control freak about using a system? Are you talking to a person who wants to save money about making money? Are you talking to a person who is talking instead of listening?

> *"The individual situation doesn't dictate the outcome.*
>
> *The person with the greatest influence does."*

In other words, are you wasting your breath because you haven't built rapport? We'll dive into specific rapport-building techniques later. For now, let's break down the Personality Pyramid so we can know who we're talking to. Those categories are Comfort Zone, Personality Traits, Work Status, Social Status, and V.A.K.

Comfort Zone has four designations:

1- Must Be Liked: Above all else, they must retain the feeling of being liked. They must have the feeling that they are accepted. They will lie or fail to share the truth with someone rather than perceive or experience the loss of acceptance or friendship. Being part of the group is more important than any other attribute for them.

2- Must be comfortable: Above all else, they must retain the feeling of being comfortable. They must feel that they are operating within their current comfort level. Their conscious mind will resist all growth until they feel comfortable enough to move forward. At this stage, they cannot risk stepping out of their comfort zone mentally.

3- Must Be Right: Above all else, they must retain the feeling of being right all the time. Being wrong is not an option. They must, more often than not, have the last say in a conversation. Often, they will say things like, "I know," "I did that," or "I say that." They are never to blame for anything, not even their own actions, no accountability. They rarely take responsibility for anything negative.

4- Must Win: Above all else, they must retain the feeling of being the winner in the conversation or feel they won you over to their way of thinking. Debating, arguing, or competing for the win of a conversation or viewpoint is in their nature. Proving their point or way of thought is a must because they have to feel as though they "won" any kind of challenge, confrontation, or disagreement.

Personality Traits has four designations:

1- Sanguine: This is the chatty-social type. They get along well with almost anyone. They can get others excited about issues. They are motivated by fun and good times. Hence, they are not always the most reliable for getting things done. They love being with people, do not like being alone, and are very emotionally expressive. They make great event hosts. They wear their heart on their sleeve and usually support the underdog in social situations.

2- Melancholy: This is the mental type. Their behavior will involve thinking, assessing, making lists, and evaluating the positives and negatives of every aspect before making a decision, widely known as the engineering mindset. They are highly talented and often brilliant, which is why it is difficult to help them get out of their own way. They usually think they are the smartest person in the room, almost any room. However, many times, they experience paralysis by analysis. They feel the need to do things the right way or not do them at all.

3- Phlegmatic: This is the flat type. They are very easy-going and laid back. They are characterized as nonchalant, relaxed, and even unexcitable. They aim for and desire peace. They are neutral people, often going with the status quo. They only upset people with their inability to make a decision. It's like pulling teeth when it's time for them to make a tough decision. It's almost impossible for them to choose between two bad things as they don't want anything bad to happen to anyone. They care about people and harmony in every situation.

4- Choleric: This is the commander-type, born leader. They are confident, dominant, strong, and stubborn. They are able to make decisions quickly and are not afraid to act. They think in the big picture format. They will sacrifice themselves for the larger team. Their main focus is getting things done. They have no problem hurting a few feelings to ensure the growth of that person or the success of an endeavor. They are less concerned with feelings than results. Their assertiveness is often misinterpreted as aggressiveness, and their confidence is often times confused with arrogance. They believe the end justifies the means and will get things done, regardless.

Work Status (Kiyosaki-Cashflow Quadrant) has four designations:

1- Employee: *Mindset is security*. Being an employee is a great place to start life, but many times, it is not a good place to end up, as employees cannot survive on savings. Their main concerns are a steady paycheck and benefits. Their idea of investing is the company 401K plan. They are conditioned to swap hours for dollars and, therefore, have a ceiling on their income. One life focus is retirement savings. You will hear self-pride swell in their voice when they tell you how hard they work, or how they have more than one job, or how long they have been on their job. One statement you will hear them say often is that they were told if they worked hard, they could have the lifestyle they desire, which we know is just not true. However, they cling to such statements to justify their belief.

2- Self-Employed or Specialist: *Mindset is control*. These are your Doctors, Lawyers, Contractors, and Consultant, generally, people who want to be the boss or just don't want to be the employee. They want to control more of their trade skill, time, or money. They often find themselves working harder and more hours than they did as an employee. Unfortunately, they are still swapping hours for dollars. They have to do all the work or reduce their profits by hiring employees. One life focus is managing overhead costs.

3- Big Business: *Mindset is the bottom line.* They want more money with less involvement. They want leverage, more specifically, time leverage of others. Generally, they have 500 or more employees. For networkers, that would be 500 or more teammates, downline. Most big businesses enjoy huge tax advantages but also suffer huge overhead. An exception to the rule is a large home-based or online business with not much overhead. The main focus is profit and loss.

4- Investor: *Mindset is returns.* This is when your money is working for your money rather than YOU working for your money. They seek high ROIs with as little risk management as possible. They know the larger the risk, the larger the return. They swap dollars for dollars, not hours for dollars. They ask a lot of questions and rarely make nonsensical excuses. One main focus is their time freedom.

Social Status has four designations:

1- Poor: *Keyword is survival.* This is a mentality, not how much cash they have in their pockets. This type of person usually has a victim mentality. They believe their circumstances determine their lifestyle. They survive from day to day emotionally and financially. Since they feel that they are a victim of circumstances, their situation is not their fault, so there is little accountability. They often have no way out of this mindset without the direct influence of a mentor.

2- Broke: *Keyword is work.* They live paycheck to paycheck. They believe the more they work, the better quality of life they will have. Or they give up on their dreams and settle for the best version of life they can have. People often confuse Poor and Broke. This is not a mentality but a situation easily remedied by beginning to work smarter, not longer, or harder. They often lack resources because they do not network; they just work. Their perceived value of self and others is preceded by a prestigious job title. They rate their personal value and the value of others on rank or job length.

3- Rich: *Keyword is lifestyle.* They live to not outlive their money. Most are looking for low-risk income opportunities and investments solely for the purpose of not outliving what they have accumulated. They MUST maintain their lifestyle or perception of an above-average lifestyle. Often, they make decisions that force them to live slightly beyond their means. More money coming in gives them a false sense of security. Most have refinanced their homes. This mentality is known as 'Keeping Up with the Jones'. Their concerns are personal, health, and travel. Often, their entire life can revolve around loved ones such as their family, children, or grandchildren.

4- Wealthy: *Keyword is Whatever.* They live a "Whatever" lifestyle. They do whatever they want to do, whenever they want to do it, wherever they want to do it, with whomever they want, even if they have to pay for it all. They have paid the price for success and are reaping what they have sown. They can be selfish. They can be over-critical camouflaged as honesty. Their main concern is long life.

V.A.K. has three designations:

1- Visual: They process in images and usually speak at a quick pace. They associate ideas, data, concepts, and other information with images and techniques. They understand a topic better when shown graphs, maps, charts, illustrations, or the company product itself. They are usually hands-on learners. Most have an excellent sense of direction. The vast majority of people are visual learners; hence, the reason television is widely preferred over radio.

2- Audio: Auditories process using sounds. They may struggle when they read information but have complete understanding as they listen to a speaker. They will speak out loud when memorizing because they need to hear it. They may move their lips or speak aloud to themselves when they read or concentrate on a task. Sometimes, they can allow their emotional sense to override their logical sense.

3- Kinesthetic: They process in a physical manner. They learn by doing or by being involved. Many are close talkers. They have a need for physical touch and, therefore, can be the touchy-feely type. They must hold items to really understand them. They have unusually high hand-eye coordination and are adept at multitasking.

Every person has more than one trait in each category. We all have a positive and a negative. We may display multiple traits within a particular category; however, one trait will always be dominant. You can learn to identify these individual dominant traits and guide the conversation for peak understanding and compliance.

For example, let's presume you need someone to clean their bedroom, take you to run some errands, want an employee to complete a project, need a client to make a favorable decision, or want a customer to buy something from you.

How do you guide that conversation in a way that is mutually beneficial to all parties involved? Remember, a successful transaction is one that ensures all parties get something they want; if not, the agreement may not be solid or long-lasting.

The individual situation doesn't dictate the outcome; the person with the greatest influence does. Stop having conversations with their conscious mind and have a deeper, more meaningful conversation with their subconscious mind.

For the highest percentage of success, you should find their WHY, then, through your rapport-building process, identify their dominant traits, have the conversation with their subconscious using linguistic patterns, tap into their decision-making process, and attach something they want to what you want. Fortunately, we will cover each of these skill sets in depth later.

> *"By identifying and speaking directly to their dominant traits,*
> *you're tapping into their decision-making process, their subconscious."*

Let's say you want your direct supervisor to give you more responsibility, and you have identified them to have the dominant traits of a Visual-Rich-Self-Employed-Phlegmatic-Must Be Liked.

Without thinking, you would know a Visual trait would require hearing trigger words such as "See" or "Look." The Rich trait would need to hear that others are doing it or other people get what they want by doing it. The Self-Employed trait requires them to know they have a measure of control, even if it's only "perceived" control. The Phlegmatic trait would need to be addressed with the feeling of ease and that there is a resulting peace in the agreement, that everyone will be happy. The Must Be Liked trait will need to be reassured by hearing that the proposed agreement will make them shine, be more popular, or make them more desirable in the eyes of those they respect.

One version of that message could be conveyed with this kind of language: "Ms. Supervisor, as you can see, I have the time management necessary to keep up with all of my duties and have noticed that other successful supervisors give their employees more responsibility because it fosters teamwork among workers and gives you more control over how quickly tasks get done, which takes the pressure of deadlines off the table, all while validating that you're an efficient and effective supervisor. I mean, what if your department had a positive jump in productivity because your staff began working together in unprecedented ways? Would that be awesome? Your supervision and input would be welcomed, and everyone would feel like they are growing by cross-training, making each team member feel more valued and raising team morale. If these were options, which would be the first area you'd like me to pitch in and help with: data entry or front desk?"

Could you respond with a simple "No"?

Correct me if I'm wrong, but the supervisor/manager has been backed into a corner that requires them to respond positively and affirmatively because if they don't, then there must be an undisclosed bias. By identifying and speaking directly to their dominant traits, you're tapping into their decision-making process, their subconscious.

These dominant traits in each category show us what we believe. Our statements reveal how and what we think. If we pay attention, we can see the thought process behind decisions. They show our highest values, what's important to us, which relates to what we have and what kind of lifestyle we live.

This personality pyramid can help you identify who you are talking to because you can learn the mind and mindset of the brain/person with whom you are communicating. You'll know them on a deeper level.

You'll be speaking in such a way that you're addressing the individual traits of the person or people, and you may be able to lead them where you need them to be, mentally, physically, or both.

In other words, you can influence their decision-making process when you know their highest values by building rapport on the subject matter that's important to them. You can allow people to know, like, or trust you when you know who you're talking to. This is rapport building. This is leadership. This is influence.

Dr. John C. Maxwell says, "Everything rises and falls on leadership." Not some things. Not a few things. Not the important things. Not the minor things. Everything. Everything you ever want to achieve or obtain requires the cooperation and involvement of other people. Does it make sense to you to learn how to effectively speak to or influence others?

These topics can get deep and technical. There is so much information coming in from the five senses that govern our human nature that our brain only processes information that we can relate to. The information we cannot relate to, don't understand, or don't immediately need gets filed away in the subconscious until it's needed in the future.

In the movie The Matrix, Neo was sitting on a park bench speaking with the Oracle, and she said something I'll never forget. To paraphrase, she explained things to Neo, and he said he didn't understand. So, she told him, the human mind needs to keep things simple, and we are unable to process a decision that we ourselves wouldn't make. This was life-changing for me.

Have you ever witnessed a situation, maybe from a distance or in passing, of a person being treated badly and said to yourself, "That couldn't be me. I would have done this or that"? We cannot process why that man/woman stays with that abusive woman/man. We don't understand why that friend or relative stays on with that horrible company. If we wouldn't make the same decision under the same circumstances, then it's difficult to understand why someone else would.

Each generation has become more skeptical, cautious, and guarded. Generally speaking, the Internet age has created a dynamic of "research and verify." Have you noticed when you say something someone doesn't agree with, they say they'll go "research it" or "google it"?

"...knowledge is not key; the application of knowledge is key."

We are naturally more suspecting of each other nowadays. Our minds are a bit closed to things we don't easily accept. This closure of our mind limits our understanding of other individuals and some life situations. We cannot help them or learn from the situation because we are too wrapped up in ourselves and our own thoughts as we fail to get out of our own way.

A training that I have delivered many times is called "The Dance and The Science Behind It." It is a very long, involved, explanatory, and technical training. It's sixteen hours in total. It's the size of an online college course, so we can only go so deep for the purpose of this book. That said, we will be looking at specific "How To" information you can use today, right now, so buckle up!

The information in The Dance is beyond life-changing. I cannot completely express how much my life has changed since acquiring this knowledge. I am so grateful to have witnessed the lives of thousands of people change for the better in dozens of different ways simply by understanding and implementing the information in these trainings.

They say knowledge is key. I disagree. Having knowledge is useless if you don't use it. I say knowledge is not key; the application of knowledge is key. I said it before, and I'll say it again. If you apply what you learn within these pages, you will have the opportunity to enhance your life tremendously.

For those of you reading this material but are not in the direct sales industry, please understand this information also applies to you. You'll have the ability to turn a conversation in the direction you want it to go. You'll have a successful blueprint for de-escalating out-of-hand situations. You'll have the confidence to say yes when you mean yes and say no when you mean no without offending anyone.

Additionally, as the customer, you can recognize how you're being handled in any transaction or situation. You can utilize the same techniques the salesperson uses with you to change the tide of negotiations.

If you implement these techniques, it is much easier for you to get your child to do their homework, do their chores, or behave in a way that is desirable to you. Your relationships, whether personal or professional, will be enhanced because they will be more productive, fulfilling, and satisfactory.

The Dance training begins with this statement; "With this training, you will learn "How To" Persuade, Influence, and Lead people to achieve THEIR needs, wants, and desires. Then and only then will you be able to achieve YOUR needs, wants, and desires. Remember, change is usually painful, so hold on to WHY you are willing to change."

I'm sure you noticed the words in all caps. I'm not yelling; I'm emphasizing. Hopefully, you will be impacted as hard as I was as we explore "The Dance."

> *"The domino effect alone, of achieving goal after goal after goal,*
> *will positively affect other areas of one's life."*

The Dance is timeless. The Dance has been done in every Arena, in every company, in every industry, in every continent, in every country, in every state, in every city, in every town, in every home, in every classroom, in every meeting, and in every relationship. The Dance has been done by everyone, from newborns to the elderly. We've all done The Dance at one time or another. The Dance has been done since the beginning of time and will be done until the end of time, guaranteed. The Dance is timeless.

What exactly is The Dance? The Dance is Persuasion. Persuasion, by definition, is the act of persuading, the act of *influencing* the mind by arguments or reasons offered, or by anything that *moves* the mind or passions or *inclines* the will to a determination. "Persuasion is the act of persuading someone to do something or to believe that something is true." Synonyms include urging, *influencing*, conversion, *inducement*." [14]

As you can see, Persuasion is *Influence*. Influence, by definition, is to control or *move* by power, physical or moral; to affect by gentle action; to exert an *influence* upon, to modify, bias, or sway. "Power resulting from ability, wealth, or position. To have an influence upon means to affect what they do or what happens." Synonyms include to *move*, to *persuade*, to *induce*.[15]

As you can see, Influence is Leadership. Leadership, by definition, is the position or office of a leader to *influence* or *induce*; to cause. "Someone's leadership is their position or state of being in control of a group of people. Synonyms include authority, control, *influence*, command."[16] Persuasion, Influence, and Leadership all have common synonyms and are sometimes used interchangeably.

More specifically, this author defines The Dance as "the act of using the techniques of Persuasion, Influence, and Leadership to accomplish a specific set of goals." It is incredibly difficult to explain without over-explaining because of the wide-reaching power associated with these skills. The domino effect alone—achieving goal after goal after goal—will positively affect other areas of one's life.

However, as previously stated, notice the three quotes, "Using the techniques of Persuasion, Influence, and Leadership to accomplish a specific set of goals," "Everything rises and falls on Leadership,"[17] and "Almost everything we want to accomplish requires the cooperation of other people."[18] When you combine these three statements, you have the roots, the basics, the foundation of the art of moving people.

Influence is very powerful. It can be the difference between success and failure. Because I want you to understand how powerful a tool it is, I am quoting the description of the book "Power Persuasion: Using Hypnotic Influence in Life, Love and Business" by Danek S. Kaus and David R. Barron.

It states, "… Whether you want to make a sale, get a date, or receive that raise-whatever it is, you have to convince somebody to say YES. For most people, influencing others is pretty hit-or-miss. Power Persuasion: Using Hypnotic Influence in Life, Love and Business will show you the secrets of getting people to do what you want. Power Persuasion will show you how to: Have total strangers warm up to you in seconds. Discover someone's hot button for any product. Give hidden hypnotic commands and suggestions during normal conversation. Change other people's beliefs. Win every argument and still keep the relationship. Overcome objections. Convince your kids to do their homework without back-talk. Get more dates than you ever imagined. Improve all your relationships, and much, much more."[19]

This book was just one resource that went into The Dance training. It is very advanced training to help those who want to build strong, profitable, stable, long-lasting, fast-growing businesses and those who want to develop productive, resourceful, stable, long-lasting, quality relationships. Now, do you understand completely how powerful The Dance is?

I believe it was Blair Warren who, so wonderfully, summed up the way to create influence by introducing us to his One Sentence Persuasion, which states, "People will do anything for those who encourage their dreams, justify their failures, allay their fears, confirm their suspicions, and help them throw rocks at their enemies."[20]

Influence affects everything around you, from the making of government policy to who sits on the board of the companies in your local business centers. You influence and are influenced every day by family, friends, coworkers, social media, and many more. Do you understand the power that comes from understanding "the power of influence" in everyday life?

"Connecting is building rapport, ensuring understanding,
and purposely conversing with intent."

Fantastic, let's begin with Contacting versus Connecting. Contacting is saying hello. Contacting is making contact with another individual in such a way as to have a conversation. Connecting is the manner in which that conversation is being handled. It's like the difference between *speaking to* children and *collaborating with* a colleague.

Connecting is building rapport, ensuring understanding, and purposely conversing with intent. Many of us speak TO other people all the time, but we rarely speak WITH people. Speaking *to* someone is very different than speaking *with* someone. Speaking *with* someone will always yield more favorable results.

With the influence of The Dance, Contacting in simple business terms is Connecting with people to make them aware of the product, good, service, or opportunity associated with your business. In everyday life, Contacting is Connecting with people to convey a particular idea, concept, or belief while building a trustworthy relationship.

Connecting, with purpose, could be perceived as the ability to effectively communicate with people in an attempt to create a mutually beneficial relationship. In other words, customers/clients need you to provide your products, goods, services, or opportunities for their own needs and comfort. Also, you need your customers/clients to buy those same products, goods, services, or opportunities from you—mutually beneficial.

Likewise, with everyday relationships, we all have the innate desire to connect. We need to cultivate solid relationships with family, friends, neighbors, and co-workers. We also need them to reciprocate and seek us out for that same goal of relationship cultivation.

We all want to be needed, wanted, or accepted. Regardless of what we tell ourselves, being connected and wanting to be connected with is as natural and basic as breathing.

Contacting and Connecting are necessary to build any relationship and are incalculably valuable in the business world as you must, on a consistent and persistent basis, introduce or expose new people to your product, good, service, or opportunity to successfully build an organization. To summarize this point, connecting with people will afford you the greatest success in building your relationships/businesses.

It is infinitely easier and faster to obtain your needs, wants, or desires when you have the assistance and cooperation of others. Advertisement is one of many ways businesses contact and connect with new clients and existing customers/clients.

In everyday life, we advertise by what we wear, how we carry ourselves (appearance), how we conduct ourselves (voice and actions), how we respond to others (reactions), and how we make or don't make eye contact, and aggressive actions (body language).

Word-of-mouth advertising is the greatest form of cooperative advertisement. It is the assistance of previous customers bringing in new customers. It is also existing friends introducing you to new friends. These new associates are additions to your resource pool. These are beneficial relationships.

Your resource pool can be needed at any time. It could be introducing a friend to a business because they will both profit from their collaboration. It could be to introduce two friends in the hopes they can assist each other with a challenge or dilemma.

Visibility to existing customers/friends/acquaintances and exposure to new clients/people/resources are keys for a person or business wanting to experience above-average success and everyday people who want to expand their pool of resources.

Your personal connection to your resource pool is your word-of-mouth power. When we connect with another person of influence simply by being available, we connect resource pools. When we tap into each other, we also have the opportunities associated with each other's resource pools.

In addition to the traditional methods of talking to another human face to face, the Internet provides new ways of reaching the masses and interacting. Remember, whether we're using social media, walkie-talkies, or smoke signals when we're chasing our dreams, we need to be focused on learning and growing to succeed in life.

"Getting started is one of the hardest parts of achieving goals."

Let's see. We all have goals. Many give up on their goals and dreams, but some of us chase those goals, and sometimes we achieve them. How do we increase our chances of reaching our goals? One way is to have S.M.A.R.T. goals.

By definition, goals are "the object of a person's ambition or effort; an aim or desired result."[21] So, if an aim is a desired result or worth a person's effort, then would you agree this is akin to your WHY? Of course, it is. This is a full circle back to WHY we do things and what we want to achieve.

What is it, or what are those needs and wants? The best way to figure that out is to start writing. Write out what you think your dreams and goals are. Excellent!

Now, ask yourself the deep questions as to why, what, how much, and how many, and find out your real WHY. And when you think you have figured out the real why, continue digging by repeating the process to get to the essence of the WHY, behind the WHY.

When you do, you can set S.M.A.R.T. goals to ensure you reach those milestones and eventually realize your goals and dreams.

What does the acronym S.M.A.R.T. stand for?

S – They must be SPECIFIC. Detailed. So they can be mapped out.

M – They must be MEASURABLE. Quantifiable. So they can be stepping stones.

A – They must be ATTAINABLE. Possible. So they can actually be achieved.

R – They must be REALISTIC. Significant. So they can motivate you.

T – They must be TIMELY. Scheduled. Goals without dates are just dreams.

Like Kurt Thomas said, "I feel that the most important step in any major accomplishment is setting a specific goal. This enables you to keep your mind focused on your goal and off the many obstacles that will arise when you're striving to do your best." Getting started is one of the hardest parts of achieving goals.

We all want to achieve our goals sooner rather than later. An excellent first step is to take the time in the beginning to write out those goals. Identify them in such a way as to systematically go through each challenge or stage and have continual movement toward your end goal.

Challenges will arise. Technology may even come into play, and you may find a way to achieve a stepping stone quicker or more effectively. You may find additional information that requires you to insert a step on your path to success. As challenges present themselves, you have to have the discipline necessary to stay focused and keep pushing through.

Paul Meyer shared, "Crystalize your goals. Make a plan for achieving them and set yourself a deadline. Then, with supreme confidence, determination, and complete disregard for obstacles and other people's criticisms, carry out your plan." S.M.A.R.T. goals are one of the tools that successful people use to achieve their goals.

Once you have identified your WHY and even the WHY behind the WHY, you have set up your SMART goals to have an identified path to achievement. Now, it's a question of learning how to get there. If we had all the necessary information and skills, we would all be successful already, correct?

We have found that we all learn new things in different ways. We process information differently. The training I developed and used to identify the path of learning has several components. It's the same method we all used to learn how to eat, walk, talk, ride a bike, read, and excel in sports or academics, and it's the same for success in everyday life and business. That training is titled "Believe, Learn, Practice, and Teach," and it is detailed inside "The Personal Success Wheel." Please pay attention. This is a golden key to your success.

"They say perception is reality. It's not.

Perception is simply how one views reality. Reality is reality."

The Personal Success Wheel will show you how you learn, how you process information, how you grow, how you can achieve your goals, and how you can help others do the same. Personal development is the key to all success in all ways, and that begins with what you BELIEVE.

If we don't rise up to meet a challenge, we will always fall short. Success is not inside of our comfort zones. Success resides just beyond our grasp, so personal growth is necessary. What we believe is true to us. What you believe is true to you. What I believe is true to me.

You may believe the earth is round, and I may believe it's flat. We will both make decisions based on our individual beliefs. They say perception is reality. It's not. Perception is simply how one views reality. Reality is reality. We believe what we are programmed and conditioned to believe until we disrupt that programming and conditioning, ultimately modifying that belief.

For example, let me ask you a question. What is the opposite of success? The vast majority of people believe failure is the opposite of success. We have been programmed to believe that, but it simply is not true. Failure is the partner of success. One cannot succeed without failing first.

Ask the most successful people how they became successful, and they will tell you a story littered with failures. Learning from what doesn't work and expounding on what does work creates success. You cannot avoid failure. It's part of the process of becoming successful.

Many believe that if you are not succeeding, then you are failing. Again, this simply is untrue. Failure actually teaches us what doesn't work, and as we learn from these failures, we learn what does work. Failure is part of the success process, not the end of it.

The opposite of success is not working, not moving forward, and giving up—failure is quitting. If you are moving forward, making attempts to achieve a goal, then you are in the process of accomplishment. Little failures along the way are just path adjustments to building something strong and stable. These little failures are not endings; they are course corrections. One cannot accomplish goals without failures.

Believing is paramount. Look at the word UNBELIEVABLE. If we remove BELIEV, then we are left with UN and ABLE. If you are UN-ABLE to believe, then you are UN-ABLE to put forth the effort necessary to succeed—because you have to see it *mentally* before you can see it *physically*. You have to see it in your *mind* before you can see it in your *hand*. If you are UN-ABLE to believe it, then you are UN-ABLE to achieve it.

The Personal Success Wheel begins with the several components of Believe, Learn, Practice, and Teach. So, it all starts with BELIEVE. You must *believe* that you can achieve, or there is no sense in going forward. *Learn* how to achieve it, *Practice* the skills necessary to achieve it, and then *Teach* it to others. This process is how we learned how to do everything. Oh, you want proof. Okay.

Those of you with younger siblings, children, nieces, and nephews, remember how we watched the children begin to want to feed themselves instead of being fed? They reached for the spoon and turned their head away because they wanted to feed themselves. When you let them, they had food in their ears, nose, and eyes. This was the Belief phase.

This is the same as learning to ride a bike or drive a car. We see others do something so many times that we *believe* we can do it, too. When we attempt it, we find out that we're not so good at it, and it's not as easy as it looked when we saw others doing it. This is the Learning phase.

We continue to attempt to feed ourselves, we fall down on the bike and get back up, we get behind the wheel and freeze with panic, or we go so slowly that our fear is evident. As we continue attempting, we are in the Practicing phase. Practicing over and over again, we absorb new abilities.

We add new information and skills to our repertoire during the process of Believing, Learning, and Practicing. The best way to reinforce the fundamentals in ourselves is to Teach those same skills to others.

Just like when we learned to feed ourselves, we began feeding everything: the doll babies, the little military guys, the fish, the turtle, everything, right? It was the same as when we learned how to walk; we immediately tried to teach the family pet and the dolls. Same thing. This is how we master new talents; *teaching* them to someone else reinforces the fundamentals in ourselves.

> *"...we started listening to ourselves and stopped doing the very process*
> *that has made us successful so many times."*

The process of Believe, Learn, Practice, and Teach is how we learned to do everything successfully as a child. However, as we got older, we started listening to ourselves and stopped doing the very process that has made us successful so many times. Let's get ourselves out of our own way.

For business owners—in other words, all of us (because we treat ourselves like a business, right?):

Believe: You must convince yourself that your dreams and goals are attainable, and then you'll be able to take action to see those dreams and goals come to fruition. You must be able to visualize yourself in the act of succeeding or accomplishing. You must have a mental picture of your dreams and goals. You have to be able to see it (mind) before you see it (hand).

Learn: New concepts, strategies, and techniques, including the latest technology, as well as proven traditional strategies, to ensure the achievement of your dreams and goals.

Practice: You will need a specific skill set to Persuade, Influence, and Lead. Learn these techniques and practice them until they are part of you. And when you think you have mastered those techniques, Practice them some more.

Teach: When you have truly mastered the recipe for success, teach it to others. Only through the process of duplication can you exponentially multiply your efforts.

As we stack our newly learned skill sets to create a firm foundation for success, we are repeating the process continually. It's a wheel, your Personal Success Wheel. It's how we become Unconsciously Competent, which also has four phases.

Phase one is akin to the Believe Phase; it's when we are Unconsciously Incompetent.

Phase 1: *Unconscious Incompetence* (you don't know that you don't know) – This is when you don't know how to do something, and you don't realize that you don't know how to do it.

Phase 2: *Conscious Incompetence* (you NOW know that you don't know) – This is when you come to the realization and admit you don't know how to do something correctly. This is the Learn phase.

Phase 3: *Conscious Competence* (you NOW know that you NOW know) – This is when you hesitate and struggle through doing something correctly but can do it only with concentrated focus. This is the Practice phase.

Phase 4: *Unconscious Competence* (you know that you know that you know) – This is when you can do something correctly without a moment of thought or hesitation. This is the Teach phase.

These phases will assist in the process of reaching your dreams and goals. As you can see, it all begins with belief. When you truly **believe**, you will get you into action. Taking **action** is the only way to get results. Those **results** will increase your confidence over time as you become Unconsciously Competent with your list of S.M.A.R.T. goals. That **confidence** will, in turn, increase your **belief**, giving you what you need to take bigger **action**. Of course, this will yield bigger **results** and further increased **confidence**. The wheel continues. So, take note, Believe, Action, Results, and Confidence is another wheel inside of your Personal Success Wheel.

Another wheel is Yourself, Systems, Tools, and Events. One who believes in *themself* or at least the process can plug into systems that are available to assist in achieving their goals. There are a number of systems available in every industry, including childrearing.

Systems are proven methods of success that allow a person the opportunity to skip a few mistakes by learning from others. This is called wisdom. Smart is learning from your own mistakes; wisdom is learning from the mistakes of others. The same applies to the tools of a trade.

Not all *tools* are useful at all stages of development. By plugging into systems and using the same tools as those who have already become successful, one can enjoy a reduction in time and costs using what has already been proven to work.

The experience and growth provide the confidence to attend the *events* necessary to network within a particular industry. It is all related, and all success is a continual process.

The last wheel is Self-Growth, Team Growth, Exponential Growth, and Residual Income. Self-Growth is imperative. Our incomes are commensurate with our personal development (*Self-Growth*).

As we believe, learn, and grow, we become aware of the resources around us. That's when we begin to increase our network (*Team Growth*).

Our network of resources will afford us all we need to get into exponential growth. We cannot do it alone. We need a team. We need to surround ourselves with people who have talent and experience that we don't have (*Exponential Growth*).

It is almost impossible to get into exponential growth without team growth. It is equally difficult to create residual income without exponential growth first, also known as momentum (*Residual Income*).

We all have the opportunity to capitalize on the cycles in our lives. If we recognize them and use them as intended, to Believe, Learn, Practice, and Teach, then we will go through the processes that lead to success.

Remember, success leaves clues. I believe that's why we say, "You can't hide money." What someone achieves, someone else can duplicate. It is much more difficult to blaze a path than to follow well-worn steps. Hence, success leaves clues.

Predictable results come from proper preparedness. If we learn what works and disregard what doesn't, then we increase our likelihood of success. To do that, it is important to follow and learn. All the best leaders were once great followers.

"With rapport, all goals are achievable. Without it,
your Dreams and Goals are a difficult uphill climb."

Once we focus on networking, we will begin to expand our comfort zone, increase our resource pool, and develop the skills necessary to obtain and maintain success. This learning journey of connecting with others, persuading, influencing, and leading begins with the ability to create rapport.

Back to The Dance. Rapport is defined as an emotional bond or friendly relationship between people based on mutual liking, trust, and a sense that they understand and share each other's concerns. Synonyms for Rapport are Relationship, Understanding, Bond, and Connection.

How do you accomplish this? Above all else, remember that rapport is the foundation of Persuasion, Influence, and Leadership. Rapport is the most powerful tool in your arsenal. With rapport, all goals are achievable. Without it, your dreams and goals are a difficult uphill climb.

Genuinely caring for the well-being of another allows you to uplift, encourage, and edify others to promote familiarity and connection. It's necessary that others understand you. What sense is a conversation if the parties involved do not comprehend the message being conveyed?

Speaking someone's language allows for greater understanding, fostering faster rapport. Speaking someone's language is more than English, Spanish, or French; it's the language of their subconscious. You have to engage in assertive communication.

"Assertive communication increases satisfaction and likelihood of achieving goals. By using assertive communication techniques, you are more likely to achieve a desired outcome because your wants and needs are more clearly understood. In addition, people are more likely to listen attentively and respond positively if they feel their needs and desires are also being respected, which is a product of assertive communication."[22]

Rapport is casting a spell on yourself and the person with whom you're speaking. You cannot only cast the spell on them; you must feel it, too. Rapport is being "in sync," "on the same page," or "connecting" with someone. It is more than just understanding. It's you feeling what they feel. It's connecting one soul to another.

People like people who are like themselves. However, liking someone is not the same as being in rapport with someone. Be careful; you can be in rapport with someone you dislike. You cannot create in-depth rapport without absorbing a bit of the essence of the people you connect to. As you create rapport and connect, beware that you do not let too much of someone rub off on you unless it's a good trait.

"...help people understand the meaning you are attempting to convey."

A Quick Word on Intonation Patterns: "It's not what you say; it's how you say it." We have all heard this before. This is crucial when you are speaking with others. Emphasizing certain words—with voice fluctuation—is a very powerful tool.

Placing a strategic or dramatic pause after a word also creates emphasis and can help people understand the meaning you are attempting to convey. So many of us THINK people understand what we are saying, and that may be true, but do they understand what we MEAN to say?

Let's illustrate this point using this one sentence, "I NEVER SAID HE TOOK IT." Read it again. Read it again. Okay, nothing miraculous, right? Now, go through the sentence again putting emphasis on each word and a pause after that emphasized word.

Does the meaning of the sentence change and become clearer?

For example, what comes to mind when you hear someone say, "I never **SAID**, he took it," as opposed to, "I never said **HE**, took it"?

Read these two sentences again aloud, putting the emphasis on the word "SAID" with a pause and then emphasizing the word "HE" with a pause.

If you actually did as instructed, did you hear this one sentence just give you two different meanings?

The first sentence that emphasizes the word "SAID" implies that he never actually said the words that he took it. He may have gestured with his eyes, pointed his hand, or nodded his head, to indicate who took it but never SAID that he took it.

The second sentence that shows the inflection on the word "HE" implies that the person in question, HE, may not have taken it, but someone else took it. "I never said HE took it because Alice took it."

These two sentences deliver two different meanings even though the words in the sentence are exactly the same. We can make what we are attempting to say easier to understand by using voice inflections and changing our intonation patterns.

Otherwise stated, putting emphasis and pauses on certain words and in different places in a sentence changes the sentence's meaning and can be easier for someone to understand. The ability to influence others is exponentially increased as well because rapport is built on the subconscious level.

There are many techniques associated with building rapport, i.e., Mirroring and Matching. Building rapport can be uncomfortable. Be willing to be a little uncomfortable to help others be more comfortable with you. It's about them, not you.

Rapport techniques work because even though they are unaware of it (on a subconscious level), the other person is thinking, "Wow, he or she is just like me." Again, people like people who are like themselves.

Start with creating the habit of sharing a warm greeting with everyone you meet or speak to. A greeting can speak volumes. A warm smile, saying hello, a handshake, and making eye contact are all parts of a successful greeting.

Being in the people business, I have taken many phone calls. I always notice when someone asks me how I'm doing but continues the conversation without allowing me to respond to that particular question. It's because they were not really interested in how I was doing. They are simply going through the motions of their insincere greeting.

Be happy and enthusiastic. No one wants to be around a bore. They can be bored to tears at their job. People follow people, not companies. Be worth following. Be honest, sincere, and real. People can feel it if you are incongruent. People are uncomfortable around people who are inconsistent. The best version of you will certainly outshine your best imitation of someone else.

Find common interests. Ask questions and be genuinely interested in the answers. Then, show that interest with follow-up questions. People don't care how much you know until they know how much you care. Be genuine. i.e., ask about their life, health, dreams, kids' names, and their likes and dislikes. Using rapport techniques helps you get out of your own way.

Being Unconsciously Competent in building rapport allows you to focus on what THEY are thinking and not what YOU are thinking and doing. In other words, you will begin to pay more attention to others than self. People like that kind of special attention. They will want to be around you more often and be more receptive to what you're offering.

Sensory modes play a large role in building rapport. Understanding sensory modes will help you increase rapport quickly. You can do this by "Matching" another's language to promote a better understanding of your topic. Rapport and sensory modes are based on Neurolinguistic Patterns or NLP.

"...this preferred Sensory mode reflects how

their brain processes information."

NLP was developed by Richard Bandler and John Grinder when they began studying the relationship between the brain and language. They found that everyone has a preferred sensory mode. More importantly, they found this preferred sensory mode reflects how their brain processes information. Sometimes, people switch or combine sensory modes, but usually, one is dominant.

Visual people think in pictures. In conversations, they might say, "I see what you mean," "It's clear to me," or "That's a bright idea."

Auditory people process the sounds of things. They want to verbalize their thoughts. "That sounds good," "It rings true," or "I hear what you're saying."

Kinesthetic people are into their feelings, literally. They want something to "feel good," "get a handle on something," or "have a gut feeling." They also prefer to touch or handle things rather than to look at them or talk about them.

A Quick Word on Presentations: As I referenced earlier in "Knowing Who You're Talking To," Visual people want to see pictures of the product or opportunity and, if possible, the product or opportunity itself, preferably demonstrated. They find graphs, charts, and pictures more convincing than your words.

Auditories will prefer to hear what you have to say and will note how you say things. Do you speak with an air of authority and confidence, or does your voice betray uncertainty, fear, or deception? In some cases, even a video does not and cannot satisfy this sensory mode.

Kinesthetics will want to touch the product, hold the brochure, or feel the chart. Let them. They need to hold it (not read it) to understand it. This presents a challenge with online presentations.

A successful group presentation will have all the elements necessary to satisfy all three sensory modes abundantly. Not speaking someone's sensory language will surely create a feeling of indecision or even lead to miscommunication.

As you begin to build rapport, you will begin to build relationships that could and should form genuine friendships or business relationships with a foundation built on mutual trust.

Voice Matching is a major factor in rapport building. In regard to how fast we talk, let's dive into Speed. Begin by listening to how fast someone speaks and gradually adjust how fast you speak to match them.

Not only does this make people feel more like you (which is rapport), but it also helps them process information at a rate at which they are comfortable. With Visuals, speak quickly because they are attempting to keep up with the ever-changing images in their minds.

However, Auditories, more often than not, tend to speak at a moderate pace and with a more sonorous (loud, deep, rich, or full) voice. Additionally, Kinesthetics speak extremely slowly as they assess their feelings and gather their thoughts. They like when something grabs them or they can see something come together/take shape. You can avoid frustrations, especially with prospects, by "Matching" their speech speed.

The goal is to create rapport, and you can do this by "Matching" another's patterns to create clearer meaning and easier acceptance of your topic. It also includes your Tone, Volume, Accent, and Breathing.

Tone: Few people speak in a monotone voice. Our voices naturally go up and down in tone during conversation. 'Matching' that rhythm will also increase rapport.

Volume: Notice the volume in which other people speak and "Match" it. When someone speaks in a loud, booming, or low, softened voice, you adjust and do the same.

Accents: The key is to listen to the vowels. Mastering another's accent is extremely flattering. It gives people a sense of "being known," which we all want deep down inside. Remember to "Match," not mimic.

Breathing: When you breathe like another person, you are "Matching" them on a primordial level. The elements to observe are the rate or rhythm and depth. "Match" it.

Remember, the purpose is to make them feel comfortable, not you.

Let's continue our dive and explore Values.

Values are the things most important to us, individually. Values move people. In conversations, notice when they light up or come alive. Notice the words used. This is the moment when they can tell you their Needs, Wants, and Desires.

Their Values: Their highest values can be learned if you ask 'what' or 'how,' not 'why.' You ask, 'what and how' to learn the 'why.' Learning someone's values allows you to attach those values to your topic.

For instance, knowing someone's highest value allows you to use it as an example or tell a story that includes their highest value, which in both cases would help them resonate with what you are meaning to say.

Showing them how your topic, product, or opportunity will fulfill their highest value, that thing they most treasure, can make your topic, product, or opportunity almost irresistible on a subconscious level. How do you learn someone's values? If rapport has been built, then just ask.

Quick Note: Do not forget Criteria.

Criteria are the guidelines by which people are willing to operate. Criteria govern values. Criteria are cheap, best, fast, natural, etc.

Remember, it's not what's important to you. Care about them and their values. Use their wording. Don't use the terminology that fits you or is correct; use the terminology that they will resonate with, their own words. If someone is interested in your 'pop-up toaster,' don't go on and on about the benefits of your 'toaster oven.' Talk to them about the benefits of your 'pop-up toaster.'

Do not ask people "WHY." Asking "WHY" will cause people to justify their reasoning. Do not ask "WHY" unless it's when you already know the answer and it's what you want them to say. "Why" elicits a conscious response, and "WHAT" reveals an unconscious response, which means, with "WHAT," you are reaching someone or communicating on a deeper subconscious level.

A replay of a simple example: During a conversation, it was uncovered that the person takes vitamins. Here is an actual conversation about vitamins.

I asked, "What is important to you in a vitamin?"
She answered, "Everyone should take vitamins for better health."

I asked, "What is it that vitamins can do for you that is important?"
She answered, "Higher energy and just generally feeling better."

I asked, "What would higher energy and feeling better overall do for you?"
She answered, "It would help me be more efficient and get more done."

I asked, "What results would happen if you were more efficient?"
She answered, "Getting more done would free up time to spend with my family."

Now, I discovered what is truly important to her: spending time with her family. We could keep going, digging deeper. Usually, a person's highest value will be just a word or phrase. Pay attention.

Remember to make mental notes so you can repeat their highest value back to them, using the exact words they used. Do it naturally, not like a drill sergeant parrot. If a person tells you her highest value is spending time with her family, do not tell her how your topic, product, or opportunity can give her more quality time. Tell her how they will allow her to spend more time with her family.

Once your topic is attached to their highest value in the form of a solution and rapport has been built, your closing is nothing more than confirming it by asking, "As you think about spending time with your family, and you see how this topic, product, or opportunity can give it to you, does it sound like something you'd like to do/can do/will do?"

Do not argue with someone as to why they would benefit from your topic. Simply attach their Highest Value to your solution using your knowledge of sensory modes and rapport building.

"Imagine having the ability to induce emotional states
that move people to action."

Diving deeper, let's explore State Elicitation. States move people to action. People do things because they feel strongly about something (emotion), and they try to justify those actions with logic.

Imagine having the ability to induce emotional states that move people to action. This power is called State Elicitation, which is true persuasion power. Step one to eliciting states is to create this state in yourself first. If you want someone to buy something, create a buying state in yourself. If you want someone to believe something, you must believe it yourself. This is why liars rarely build any relationships, personal or business, that stand the test of time: because they don't believe their own message. The result is buyer's remorse (regret), which kills longevity or commitment.

If rapport has been built properly, then that buying state will transfer to your audience. After building rapport, simply ask, "Have you ever seen something and really wanted it?" Or ask, "When you knew you wanted it, what did you feel at that moment?" Or ask, "When you absolutely knew you wanted it, how did you know?" At this point, be quiet and listen. Do not speak or try to clarify or elaborate. Just listen.

They will give you information in sensory terms, something they saw, heard, or felt. They may even tell you how they came about the process of that decision. Their decision-making process is vital information.

Now, describe your product, good, service, or opportunity in the same terms as their decision-making process. You are reflecting back to them their exact decision-making process. It would be incredibly difficult for them to say no to their own decision-making process. It's vital to match the process exactly. Knowing someone's decision-making process and being able to elicit their buying state is like having the combination to their brain. The VAK sequence, covered earlier, and NLPs are the keys.

Now, let's delve into Congruity. In Neurolinguistic Pattern (NLP) terms, you will have Congruity when your inner state matches your outer actions, speech, facial expressions, and body language. You have to really believe, really live, and really feel the things you are attempting to influence others to do, feel, and believe. In other words, in order to be a master persuader, a master influencer, or a master leader, you must not only walk the walk and talk the talk, but you must also feel the feel.

Have you ever met someone you thought was honest, sincere, and friendly, yet for some reason, your gut instinct screamed, "Don't trust them!?" It was because their inner state did not match their outer actions. They were incongruous. It doesn't mean they are dishonest or insincere. It could be that they were nervous, unprepared, or intimidated. Yet, you still did not trust them. If you are not sold on your product, good, service, opportunity, or team, then do not expect to sell others on your product, good, service, opportunity, or team. The alternative is to be a fake liar.

For those who are Closers (i.e., mommies and daddies), in the occupation of sales, or in a leadership position, the process of closing can be predictable, based on the 80/20 rule and its variations. If rapport has been built properly (there is mutual like and trust), and you have uncovered all of your prospect's objections and concerns, attach their highest value to the benefits of what you're offering. Then, the close is simply asking for them to move forward to a conclusion (go do, join, sign, or provide a credit card).

Walk them through the closing process. Keep them in their new comfort zone. They trust you, and you trust them, so stay with them and follow through with them to the end. Have fun. Make it meaningful. They just made a great decision to follow your lead/advice, so now is not the time to leave them alone. Give them immediate direction. Tell them exactly what they need to do next to move in the direction of their highest value. Be certain they have all they need to succeed, and of course, be sure you have their contact information if any follow-through is necessary.

"The specific construction of words and their sounds

give the patterns meaning and power."

One of the wonders of linguistic patterns is that they are predictable formations in a language. It doesn't matter whether the patterns are read or heard. The specific construction of words and their sounds give the patterns meaning and power. The rules of grammar, syntax, and semantics are actually linguistic patterns.

When partnered, rapport and linguistic patterns can be very powerful tools in the art of persuasion. I call this level of cognition in conversation "Dancing," hence the title of the training.

If a person takes the time to learn rapport-building skills until it becomes a natural occurrence and uses linguistic patterns seamlessly in conversation, then their level of influence and persuasion will increase exponentially, allowing them to "dance" with anyone on any level. Did you notice that I just used the If/Then linguistic pattern?

Let's go through a few examples of Linguistic Patterns.

Let's start with the linguistic pattern, "Have you found...?" The formula is to create a question that includes or leads to your desired outcome in the form of, Have you found?

For example, "Have you found that as you think about being more successful, the idea of reading more books like this will accelerate that success because you feel more empowered?"

"Have you found that when you think about freedom, when you think about YOUR freedom, when you think about not having a day job anymore, as your enthusiasm and optimism grow, you can apply that enthusiasm to the execution of the information in this book?"

Notice we didn't just ask, "Have you found that you want to do this?" Nor, "Have you found you want to learn more?" What we asked was, "Have you found…because you feel more empowered?" "Have you found that growing sense of optimism and enthusiasm…?"

Although thoughts, ideas, and actions are all pieces of the puzzle as associated factors and results of what one processes in their mind, ultimately, people are driven by emotions. All five of our senses are gathering information nonstop. All of that information is being processed, cataloged, and stored within each of us and is part of our decision-making process. Much of the data processed on the subconscious level is automatic. No thinking is necessary.

The subconscious mind simplifies data. Remember, the subconscious doesn't have feelings. It processes data. It's a computer, of sorts, that runs software that we call human nature and can even make routine tasks, no matter how difficult, seem like second nature. The subconscious mind is a mega-huge bulldozer, but the conscious mind is the little, tiny person in the driver's seat of that mighty force.

The subconscious mind is more powerful than many people realize. I believe it was Tony Robbins who stated it wonderfully when he said, "The subconscious mind goes beyond learning new skills. It's involved in information processing and affects everything we think, say, and do. It stores our beliefs and values, determines our memories, and monitors the information all around us, deciding what to send to the conscious mind and what to store for later. It affects every moment of our lives – and most of us don't even know it."

The emotions connected to a person's highest value are a powerful motivating force indeed because the entire process takes place in the brain on a subconscious level. If your conversation connects with them on that same level of emotional energy and not just on a certain amount of money or other intangible, then you will have connected to their subconscious where decisions are actually made and can affect them accordingly. Deep stuff!

This is an actual conversation to use as an example or reference.

Trainer: "Have you found that in order for you to have a successful home-based business, you have to have the skills and training that are needed? And someone to provide them?"

Prospect: "Yes, that makes sense. I see it all over the Internet."

Trainer: "But you're in a quandary. You cannot be successful without the training. Then how are you going to get the training, and who has the time to train you?"

Prospect: "I'll buy one of those programs on the Internet."

Trainer: "As you think about your security in retirement, which program seems like it will give you the training you need? And how do you know what training is needed?"

Prospect: "I don't. I'm going to have to do a bunch of research to figure it out. And I certainly can't quit my job until I do."

Trainer: "Have you found a real urgency to accomplish something more for your family than your job will allow? As you think about that, let me show you how you can get involved with a company that provides all the training you need to be successful."

Okay, let's get into some more Linguistic Patterns and examples.

"Would it be fair to say...?" (*Insert your desired outcome*) – This kind of question will allow you to lead the conversation because you will insert your desired outcome in the form of a question).

i.e., "Would it be fair to say the more these trainings help you learn the skills necessary to be successful, the more eager you are to *buy more trainings?*"

"Just suppose...?" (*Insert your desired outcome*) – "Just suppose" is always favorable because your prospects are not committing to anything; they just suppose your desired outcome.

i.e., "Just suppose for a moment, you've really mastered these techniques because you were willing to *buy, study, and practice these trainings* and just suppose *you're successful* with your home-based business only because these trainings can be taught to your team. That success feels pretty good, doesn't it?"

You get the idea. Let's kick it up a notch and explore Multiple Stacked Linguistics.

"What would happen if (*you name your outcome*) because (*insert their highest value*)?"

i.e., "What would happen if you *bought all of these trainings* and used them to build a large and profitable business because *you really want to retire with a 6-figure income?*"

"What would happen if (*you name your outcome*) because (*insert their highest value*)?"

i.e., "What would happen if you *bought all of these trainings* because *you want to get out of debt?*"

"Don't (*action or objection*) unless you want to (*name your outcome*)?"

i.e., "Don't *tell yourself they cost too much* unless you want to *buy this training* and become a successful training machine for your team, OK?"

"I appreciate (*intent of the objection*) and what would happen if (*new behavior*), because (*reason*) I'd be willing to (*concession*)?"

This pattern has four components to it:

- Agree with the objection
- Introduce your outcome
- Describe the reasoning
- Small concession in exchange for them agreeing to your proposal

i.e., I appreciate *you wanting to save money,* and what would happen if *you purchased more trainings* because *you need these skills to be successful?* I'd be willing to *help you choose which trainings would give you the fastest start.* Sound good?

"Yes (*you agree with the negative feature objected to*), but (*positive benefit of your proposal*), and if you're (*committed to emotion/highest value*) then (*you must be committed to proposal*)?"

This pattern has four components to it:

- You agree that the feature mentioned is negative

- You mention a positive benefit

- You mention a commitment to an emotion or highest value

- Finish with a commitment to the proposal or follow–through

i.e., "Yes, *I agree that the trainings require a financial investment,* but *with them, you have the opportunity to learn the skills you need,* and if you're *committed to enjoying the lifestyle that comes with having a successful home-based business,* then *you must be committed to purchasing the necessary trainings.* That does make sense to you, doesn't it?"

"(*Your objective*), and I appreciate (*future obstacles*). Imagine for a moment that together we/you (*overcome future obstacles*) as we/you have done in the past. Don't you feel good now?"

This pattern has four components to it:

- You state your outcome

- You agree with their objection

- Have them imagine overcoming future obstacles as they have done so in the past

- Then you ask, "Don't you feel good now?"

Obstacle: It takes too long to learn these new skill sets.

i.e., "*I want you to benefit from these trainings and be successful with your business,* and I appreciate *the time investment it takes to learn these new skill sets.* Imagine for a moment that you *learned these new skill sets by overcoming the time challenge*, as you have done in the past. D*on't you feel good now?*"

Additional Linguistic Patterns

"When would NOW be a good time… (*Insert your outcome*)?"

i.e., "When would NOW be a good time *to get started on the training* you need to be successful with your home-based business?"

"Because…" (*Whatever follows the word "Because" is a valid reason for the sentence*).

i.e., "You need to purchase this training because *it is how you are going to help your people obtain their freedom.*"

"The more you X, the more you Y."
i.e., "The more you *listen to this training,* the more you *want to practice these lessons,* true?"

"The more you X, the less you Y."
i.e., "The more you *listen to this training,* the less you *want to be without these lessons,* right?"

"The sooner you X, the quicker you Y."

"The more you X, the faster you Y."

"The faster you X, the safer you Y."

"Do you want X or Y?" (Alternate close)

"...it's inside the process that we can influence the final decision."

Watching and listening to a person using multiple stacked linguistics who truly has a caring heart and is motivated by an articulated WHY can be one of the most powerful conversations to witness on the planet, regardless of the topic. And don't even mention Nominalizations. Oops, too late. Let's explore Nominalizations.

The human mind likes to simplify things, and we know that. We take the entire decision-making process and make it a thing (a noun). Every time someone does this, they are taking away the process. We want to be a party to the process because it's inside the process that we can influence the final decision.

According to the Cambridge Dictionary, "We often form nouns from other parts of speech, most commonly from a verb or an adjective. We can then use the noun phrase instead of the verb or adjective to create a more formal style."[23] The brain simplifies, and we nominalize–replace a verb or adjective with a noun phrase in conversation, and in doing so, increase our ability to create rapport, communicate effectively, and move people to a determined will.

With nominalizations, you can turn *"a decision"* (a noun) into *"deciding"* (a verb). Likewise, you can turn *"deciding"* (process) into *"a decision"* (conclusion).

Let's say someone is deciding whether or not to join your team. You can bring that process to a conclusion by saying something like, "What information would you need to decide to join now?"

On the other hand, let's say they have already decided **not** to join your team. You can take that person back into the "process" of deciding, where they are open to suggestions by asking them something like, "How did you go about deciding that?"

As a general rule, any verb you can add -tion, -sion, -ment, -ent, -ence, -ance, -ancy, -ant, -ity, or -ize to can be a nominalization. Nominalizations are most powerful in combinations of three or more. Here are just a few.

To Decide	a Decision
The Experience	an Experience
To Communicate	a Communication
To Function	a Function, the Function of
To Close	the Close (of a deal)
To Grow	Growth
To Accept	Acceptance
To Realize	Realization
To Doubt	a Doubt
To Choose	a Choice

To get the full benefit of nominalizations, make an infinitive verb (to be, to run, to win, to succeed, etc.) your desired outcome.

i.e., "Tell me more about the doubts you have about your ability *to make a commitment* to yourself."

Constructing Nominalization Chains can be fun.

First, start with a nominalization and connect it with one of three words: *of, about, or how.*

Second, precede the next nominalization with either *"you"* or *"the."*

Last, finish with an infinitive verb as your desired outcome.

A diagram would look like this…

Nominalization – of/about/how – you/the – nominalization – infinitive verb.

OR…

You/the – Nominalization – of/about/how – nominalization – infinitive verb.

An example would be, "I know *you* will enjoy the *appreciation of* your *acceptance to learn* these trainings."

Pacing and Leading

This is a very powerful process that lets you give a series of commands or suggestions in such a manner that they are easily accepted.

A Pace is anything true that cannot be argued, a fact.

A Lead is a suggestion, command, or your desired outcome.

For your commands, suggestions, or outcomes to be readily accepted and eagerly acted upon, they must be delivered in a gradual manner.

- Fact, Fact, Fact, Command
- Fact, Fact, Command
- Fact, Command
- Command, Command, Command

"As a participant in this training, you've been looking at many words, you've been reading words, and you have probably noticed this is a very powerful training. Parts of this training are easy to understand. Some parts, like nominalizations, may seem advanced. Every part of this training is very powerful when used properly. There is a lot of information in this training to incorporate. It's easy to see how this training can help you build a successful business. Take your time, learn each skill set, and then teach them to your team, as duplication is the key to exponential growth."

As a participant in this training (Fact), you've been looking at many words (Fact), you've been reading words (Fact), and you have probably noticed this is a very powerful training (Command). Parts of this training are easy to understand (Fact). Some parts, like nominalizations, may seem advanced (Fact). Every part of this training is very powerful when used properly (Command). There is a lot of information in this training to incorporate (Fact). It's easy to see how this training can help you build a successful business (Command). Take your time (Command), learn each skill set (Command), and then teach them to your team (Command), as duplication is the key to exponential growth.

"People tend to agree with whatever follows these words and phrases."

Logically Speaking

Default logic words or phrases are: because, therefore, all of that leads to, that also causes, and justifies. People tend to agree with whatever follows these words and phrases.

"Being where you are and learning this training is similar to learning something that is very exciting because you know it's new and you know it's powerful, and all of that is justified by the fact that you can be successful and create a great deal of enthusiasm with your team. You'll notice, in doing that, it logically helps other people duplicate what you do, which naturally is what you'll be looking for anyway because it just makes sense, right?"

This paragraph may seem long and unorganized, but when you're in a conversation with someone and you have properly built rapport with them, they will kind of agree with a lot of the things you say.

Why? Because...

Future Pacing

Future Pacing is a very powerful process that incorporates the sensation of going back and forth in time, i.e., from present to future and back to present. It is a euphoric feeling that allows your client or customer to enjoy the decision they are making with you today but enjoy it in the future, in their mind right now in the present.

This technique is akin to dream-building. You help your prospect see the result of the decision they made today, as it will look in the future, by painting a very vivid picture.

"Ms. Jones, you have indicated that you want to create extra income before you retire in three years and be able to stay home with your grandchildren. Before you make any enjoyable decisions, let me ask you to take a moment and imagine yourself sitting with your grandchildren, playing with them, watching them take their first steps, and saying their first words. Notice what you say to yourself as all of you are laughing and having a fun time together. As you get the feeling of that, go back to when you made the decision to create that residual income. Now, do you like the choice you made to run with this team?"

Mind Reading

Presume what someone may be thinking and suggest it to them. You are not mind-reading, per se. You are planting the thought and then telling them they are having that thought. However, I want to be clear and ensure that you understand. Be careful; we reap what we sow.

You're obviously listening to this training. You're thinking about how incredibly powerful it is to be able to apply every one of these tools in your everyday life. As you're thinking about that, one of the things that can easily come to mind is that as you participate in this training, as you practice the techniques, and you begin to see the power that each of these concepts has, it's easy to begin to notice yourself thinking, *This stuff is truly powerful; this material has a great deal of potential and energy to it.*

We all have inadvertently done this at one time or another. We have said something like, "I bet you're thinking so and so…" or "It's not what you think." They may not have been thinking about it until that seed or thought was planted by you.

This is a very powerful tool. So, I repeat, be very careful when placing thoughts in people's minds; ONLY suggest thoughts you want people to have.

Lost Performative

A Lost Performative is a statement that describes a "judgment," "belief," or "standard" without the authority or justification for the statement itself. Still not sure? Just ask the question, according to whom?

i.e., "It's the latest fashion." OR "Everyone loves this." OR "This is perfect timing." OR "Smart people join this team." OR "Successful people believe this."

This pattern works best when you provide three things that are true facts in front of it.

You were told about this training or saw this training on the Internet (Fact).
You've come across this training somehow (Fact). You are listening to this training
or reading it right now (Fact), and you have found one of the most powerful and
profitable training courses you will ever purchase (Lost Performative).

Cause and Effect

"If *X*, then *Y*."

This is one of the easiest and most graceful language patterns because it's based on default logic and meaning.

As with all language patterns, this one relies heavily on the level of rapport.

i.e., "If you buy this training and practice it (if), then you will have much success (then)."

OR, "If you just learn a few new skills (if), then you will improve your odds of success (then)."

Some of the more common Cause and Effect words as phrases are: because – causes – kindles – creates – generates – leads to – results in.

i.e., "Continuing this training (if) will result in you having information overload (then)."

Okay, I know that was a lot of information. Some of it may still be a bit confusing. Just remember, all of these skills do not have to be learned overnight. It will take time to fold them into your daily life as new habits. The best way to do that is how? That's right, Believe, Learn, Practice, and Teach.

"...taxes can be an asset rather than continue to be a liability."

Now, you have more than enough data to prove that you should, and you could set yourself up to win by treating yourself like a business. Let's dive into aspect number one, taxes with business ownership, starting by examining the tax process itself.

We're going to cover the extreme basics of how taxes work. Oh! I forgot to start with an important statement: This design is purposeful, not coincidental. Taxes were designed to be a tool that produces income for the government; nothing more, nothing less. However, I will explain how taxes can be an asset rather than continue to be a liability.

Grab a pen and paper if necessary. This section is crucial. Seriously, if you get this part, then you have one of the golden keys to success.

Your paycheck is calculated by algorithms and mathematical formulas, all in the name of cashflow. It is measured against a chart with a breakdown of yearly incomes. Zero dollars to $9,999 is taxed at a specific lower percentage, like 10%. The next bracket may be $10,000 to $28,999 and taxed at 14%. The next could be $29,000 to $47,999, which is taxed at a slightly higher 19%. The tax chart continues like that, so every chunk is taxed at one level or another to average an overall tax.

Additionally, Medicare and Social Security will be deducted as well, even if you claim Exempt. When you add in all the different percentage chunks as well, you're looking at paying somewhere around 20%-35% in taxes for the average American.

Let's say the GROSS income of $30,000 dollars per year puts you in the average overall tax of 28.65%. The IRS program may calculate 28.65% of $30,000 divided by 26 weeks or 52 weeks, depending on whether you get paid each week or every two weeks. That is the amount they will deduct from each paycheck throughout the year, even before you get to see your money.

Now, stay with me; it gets tricky right here.

GROSS of $30,000 times 28.65% equals $8,595 dollars in tax liability, divided by 52 weeks equals $165.29 per week that will be deducted from each paycheck, so by the end of the year, the full $8,595 will be paid.

Curveball!

When you file your taxes at the end of each year, you will AT LEAST have the Standard Deduction. Many people qualify for several Deductions and Exemptions such as Childcare Credits, Head of Household, Up to 3 Children, Business Deductions, Earned Income

Credits, Education Credits, and any number of dozens of Deductions or Exemptions.

Why is this important? Because you subtract all Deductions and Exemptions from the Gross to determine your AGI, your Adjusted Gross Income, which is your ACTUAL taxable amount. The taxable amount should be multiplied by the 28.65% to determine how much you're required to pay in taxes. Ask yourself, why do they multiply it by

TAX PROCESS

Gross Income

Deductions and Exemptions

Gross – Deductions & Exemptions = AGI

AGI × Tax Bracket % = Tax Amount

Gross Income – Tax Amount = Net Income

Net Income – Living Expenses =

Discretionary Income per year

Discretionary Income per month

the GROSS?

Let's do the math using an example. A Gross of $30,000 minus the Standard Deduction of $12,000 equals $18,000. So, if we multiply $18,000 by 28.65%, we get $5,157.

This means the government made you pay $8,595 in taxes from your weekly paycheck, but you were only supposed to pay $5,157. Oh, so they give you a refund for $3,438 and make you think it's a second Christmas. Tax Refund time!

In this scenario, the true breakdown is that you paid $3,438 to the government all year long and they gave it back to you with zero interest. Who does that? Who loans interest-free money? Oh, we do.

Almost every one of us who has received a refund and didn't own a business provided the US Government with an interest-free loan. It simply means that taxes were OVERPAID, and there was a REFUND of what shouldn't have been paid in the first place. And again, with zero interest.

"...there is a cost to living in any country. We call that cost 'Taxes.'"

In his book, Lower Your Taxes – Big Time, Sandy Botkin, C.P.A., Esq. states, "While working at the IRS as a trainer of IRS attorneys, I realized that many people were overpaying their taxes due to the lack of knowledge or lack of information."

Taxes are an income for a country. People tell me that taxes are necessary for a country to fund its existence. I get that. That's why we pay what we owe, but not overpay!

I remember my first tax conversation with one of my early business mentors. I was complaining about having to pay taxes at all. He educated me that there is a cost to living in any country. We call that cost "Taxes."

Until we own our own country, we need to adhere to the rules of the country we decide to live in. He said, "Render unto Caesar what is Caesar's." That includes their laws of the land. With that being said, we know taxes are part of the framework, so we need to learn how to maneuver within those laws as best as possible.

Any financial advisor worth their fee will tell you the less tax you pay, the better off you are. Personally, I believe in the advice given by the aforementioned financial authority, Sandy Botkin. In his book, the title of Chapter 1 is "Why You Would Be Brain Dead Not to Start a Home-Based Business (If You Don't Already Have One)."

Why? Because the tax-deductions associated with a simple home-based business or online business can be incredibly significant.

Please notice he didn't say "uninformed," "unintelligent," "lack business savvy," or "stupid." He said, "BRAIN DEAD." When a former IRS attorney, who is also a certified public accountant, tells you that you would have to be brain-dead to NOT own a home-based or online business, you listen.

I listened many years ago and can tell you from firsthand experience that life is better. You have to understand that taxes are a never-ending cycle whose effects can only be minimized by jumping through the same loopholes as the huge corporations.

Tax laws are tax laws. They apply equally across the board. It does not matter if it's a mom-and-pop shop or a huge mega box store; the tax laws apply to both in the exact same way. Anyone who treats themselves like a business has access to the same loopholes as any other business.

Which do you think is easier, more beneficial, and more desirable? Get a second job and NOT SPEND your time with your family and friends; attempt to work overtime, and of course, the more you make, the more THEY TAKE, all while NOT SPENDING your time the way you want to spend your time; invest thousands IN THE HOPES of hitting the lottery for a substantial amount; go further INTO DEBT to return to school to get a better job or higher position; or PAY LESS TAXES by reading a book and listening to people who have done it?

I chose the latter. It all made sense when I finally understood that tax deductions lower our tax liability and help keep our own money in our own pockets. Let's look at the concept of deductions so you can better understand the power of tax deductibility. Again, this is one of the golden keys.

What is a Tax-Deductible Business Expense?

According to the IRS.gov website, there are three components that have to be in place.

- Any expense incurred for the purpose of gaining or producing income; AND…
- Any expense incurred with a reasonable expectation of resulting in future business; AND…
- Any expense incurred that is reasonable under the circumstances.

We were all taught to save money, right? I always heard, "A penny saved is a penny earned." Then I read a book titled Smart Business Stupid Business by Diane Kennedy C.P.A. and Megan Hughes. There was a ton of great information. Also, there was a statement that triggered my critical thinking.

The statement was, "Every dollar you save in taxes is worth more than a dollar you earn." What? How is this possible? I understand money being saved is depreciating in value if it's in the form of cash or sitting in a bank, not in a form that hedges against inflation. True, but another aspect altogether has to do with tax deductions and the savings associated with them.

She explains that if you earn $100, you'll have to pay $20 to $40 in taxes, and then you only have $60 to $80 left over. However, if you SAVE $100 in taxes, then you still have the whole $100. Hence, "Every dollar you save in taxes is worth more than a dollar you earn."

Many financial professionals will tell you that in order to maximize your financial position, you must begin by paying the legal minimum amount possible in taxes and then, legally, morally, and ethically, increase your tax deductions.

"The internet provides ready-made business opportunities,
what I call a business in a box."

The vast majority of employees receive a refund at the end of each tax year, which means that many of us are not treating ourselves like a business. I always get the same responses when I enquire. "I don't know how to start a business," and "I can't afford to start a business."

The Internet provides ready-made business opportunities, what I call a "Business in a box." Starting an online business is easy and simple and comes with step-by-step instructions. Training is usually provided as well as someone whom you can ask questions.

Now, about affordability. If you redirect the money that you are currently loaning to the government without receiving interest, then you can use those SAME FUNDS to create your own business, which will provide you with additional income and possibly significant tax deductions.

At the risk of being redundant, I'm going to stress this again as it is a crucial piece of information that you need to learn. It is obvious that we have already been successfully conditioned to pay that money (taxes) out of each paycheck. We are used to it now. If we stop giving interest-free loans yearly, we can use that same money to start our own home-based or online business. Most likely, there are available tax deductions that you have not yet explored.

Flat out, this material has eliminated the excuse that someone who has a job cannot afford to start their own home-based or online business.

Remember, the professionals suggest we pay the legal minimum in taxes by treating ourselves like a business. We have shown you how to do that with a business in a box. Time for some fun. Let's look at what Living Expenses the IRS Tax Code says can become legitimate business deductions, reducing our tax liability.

The IRS Tax Code is over 7,000 pages and includes publications and forms. In your due diligence, please go to https://www.irs.gov/ and check out the codes for yourself, as they may change from year to year.

Here is a list of a few to get you started:

- IRS Publication 463 – Travel, Entertainment, Gift, and Expenses
- IRS Topic Number: 511 – Business Travel Expenses
- IRS Publication 535 – Business Expenses
- IRS Publication 587 – Business Use of Your Home
- IRS Form 8829 – Expenses for Business Use of Your Home

Not all Living Expenses can be Tax-Deductible Business Expenses; however, historically speaking, there are enough to create significant tax deductions when dealing with a home-based or online business.

This is a list of some, not all, Living Expenses that may become Tax-Deductible Business Expenses under certain circumstances. Again, please consult https://www.irs.gov/ or a tax professional for specific allowances based on the current tax code for your specific situation.

Living/Business Expenses	Single	Married	Living/Business Expenses	Single	Married
Mortgage/Rent	$900	$800	Mileage/Auto Expenses	$5,700	$11,400
H.O.A. Fees	$150	$150	Clothing/Dry Cleaning	$600	$1,100
Utilities	$1,800	$3,500	Travel Expenses	$900	$2K
Childcare/Eldercare	$5K	$5K	Meals	$2K	$4K
Cell Phone	$800	$1,300	Gifts	$700	$1,500
Tablet/Computers	$500	$900	Tax Preparations	$350	$650
Internet Service	$800	$1K	Continuing Education	$600	$1,200
Electronics	$700	$1,200			
Software	$200	$400	Grand Totals	$22,400	$37,300
Office Equipment & Supplies	$700	$1,200			

NOTE: This list is not all inclusive, i.e., groceries, personal property taxes, vehicle payments, vehicle insurance, personal grooming, etc.... are excluded.

This list is not all-inclusive, and, in some instances, only a percentage of an expense may be tax deductible. Looking at some averages we compiled nationwide, singles spend about $22,400 per year on Living Expenses, and married couples spend approximately $37,300.

TAX PROCESS

Gross Income

Deductions and Exemptions

Gross − Deductions & Exemptions = AGI

AGI × Tax Bracket % = Tax Amount

Gross Income − Tax Amount = Net Income

Net Income − Living Expenses =

Discretionary Income per year

Discretionary Income per month

Now, you understand that when you own a business, some of your Living Expenses may qualify as Business Expenses. So, here is where that information factors in. First, let's illustrate the tax process itself. As you can see in the Tax Process image above, the Gross Income minus the Deductions and Exemptions leaves you with your AGI, which is your Adjusted Gross Income, which is your taxable income.

You multiply the AGI by the Tax Bracket Percentage, and that shows your Tax Liability. This is the amount you owe in taxes. Subtract your Tax Amount from your Gross Income, and you have your Net Income. Subtract your Living Expenses from your Net Income, and that will leave you with your Discretionary Income. Then, of course, we break it down to yearly and monthly so you can feel the full impact.

As you can see in the Living Expenses chart above, we all have the same life expenses, give or take a few. The point is you are paying these living expenses just like a business owner is. The difference is the business owner gets to deduct some and/or a percentage of those Living Expenses as Business Expenses. Let's add some real numbers and let you really feel the impact.

First, the employee:

TAX PROCESS	SINGLE EMPLOYEE
Gross Income	$34,000
Deductions and Exemptions Earned Income Credits – Head of Household Credit – Child & Dependent Credit – Child Tax Credit & Additional Child Tax Credit – Retirement Savings Contribution Credit – Affordable Care Act Credit	$6,350 + $4,050 = $10,400
Gross – Deductions & Exemptions = AGI	$34,000 – $10,400 = $23,600
AGI × Tax Bracket % = Tax Amount	$23,600 × 29.65% = $6,997
Gross Income – Tax Amount = Net Income	$34,000 – $6,997 = $27,003
Net Income – Living Expenses =	$27,003 – $22,400 =
Discretionary Income per year	$4,603
Discretionary Income per month	$4,603 ÷ 12 = $383
	DEBT ~ Cut Corners ~ Sacrifice ~ Do Without

Take the Gross Income of $34,000 and subtract all of the Deductions and Exemptions of $10,400. That leaves you with your AGI of $23,600. Multiply that AGI by your Income Tax Bracket of 29.65%, and that gives you your Tax Amount of $6,997. Subtract that Tax Amount from your Gross Income of $34,000, and you get a Net

Income of $27,003. Then subtract the Living Expenses of $22,400 from the Net Income, leaving you with a Discretionary Income of $4,603 per year. Divide the Discretionary Income by 12 months to get the Monthly Discretionary Income of $383.

This $383 per month is the amount we have to buy groceries, pay for doctor visits, pay for our car note and car insurance, and all the other things in our Living Life slice of the Time Pie. This is why so many of us have to resort to increasing credit card debt, sacrificing life basics, and just plain doing without some of the dignities in life.

Now, let's look at the employee with a Home-Based Business (H.B.B.) or an Online Business doing the Daily Business Building Activities (D.B.B.A.).

TAX PROCESS	SINGLE EMPLOYEE	SINGLE EMPLOYEE w/H.B.B. or Online Business D.B.B.A.
Gross Income	$34,000	$34,000
Deductions and Exemptions	$6,350 + $4,050 = $10,400	$6,350 + $4,050 + $22,400 = $32,800
Gross – Deductions & Exemptions = AGI	$34,000 – $10,400 = $23,600	$34,000 – $32,800 = $1,200
AGI × Tax Bracket % = Tax Amount	$23,600 × 29.65% = $6,997	$1,200 × 21.65% = $259
Gross Income – Tax Amount = Net Income	$34,000 – $6,997 = $27,003	$34,000 – $259 = $33,741
Net Income – Living Expenses =	$27,003 – $22,400 =	$33,741 – $22,400 =
Discretionary Income per year	$4,603	$11,341
Discretionary Income per month	$4,603 ÷ 12 = $383	$11,341 ÷ 12 = $945
	DEBT ~ Cut Corners ~ Sacrifice ~ Do Without	

According to IRS Tax Code, Business Owners may pay less taxes than Employees simply because many Living Expenses can become legitimate Business Deductions.

Take the Gross Income of $34,000 and subtract all of the Deductions and Exemptions of $10,400, including the Living Expenses/Business Expenses of $22,400 for a total of $32,800. That leaves you with your AGI of $1,200. Multiply that AGI times your lower Income Tax Bracket of 21.65%, and that gives you your Tax Amount of $259. Subtract that Tax Amount from your Gross Income of $34,000, and you get a Net Income of $33,741. Then subtract the Living Expenses of $22,400 from the Net Income, leaving you with a Discretionary Income of $11,341 per year. Divide the Discretionary Income by 12 months to get the Monthly Discretionary Income of $945.

As you can see, treating yourself like a business will allow you to keep more of your own money in your pocket. As illustrated, the employee with a business was left with two and a half times as much Discretionary Income as the employee without a business. This is why most business owners don't have to sacrifice the basic dignities in life.

Mind you, these numbers are representative of just the wages because the business had no income in this equation. The employee who treated themselves like a business profited, guaranteed (99.999%) because it's IRS regulated. The IRS, by code, dictates the tax loopholes. When we treat ourselves like a business, we get to use the same tax loopholes as all other businesses.

"...this book has shown you how to keep more of

your own money in your own pocket..."

One aspect we didn't cover under the tax umbrella is Tax Refunds. The IRS governs how much comes out of your check each pay period. It is based on your Gross Income. If you do the math, taxing the Gross Income is going to create an overpayment of taxes. Why? Because when you file your taxes, the IRS subtracts your Deductions and Exemptions to get your Adjusted Gross Income (AGI). Then, they use the AGI to determine your new and lower tax bracket percentage. Since they are calculating your tax liability on the lower AGI rather than the higher Gross Income, you will certainly have overpaid your taxes and are due a Tax Refund by design.

As you can see, a Tax Refund is actually the IRS returning the amount of taxes we shouldn't have paid in the first place. In effect, this is us giving the US Government an interest-free loan. They use our money all year to make investments, make billions of dollars, and give us back the money (taxes) that we should not have even paid.

So, now this book has shown you how to keep more of your own money in your own pocket by paying the legal minimum in taxes rather than giving the government an interest-free loan.

And two, it has shown that having a home-based business or online business can create additional deductions that result in substantial tax savings, increasing your personal finances.

Now, what you need to know is how to choose a home-based business or online business that is right for you and your family. This book isn't going to attempt to sell you on an opportunity. If you feel this information is warranted, then I encourage you to do your due diligence.

The professionals suggest you choose something that you are passionate or knowledgeable about already. What excites you? What do you like to do? What would you like to do? What would you like to help other people do? What are your hobbies?

Do you like to travel? Start an online travel business. Travel and tell others about starting their own online travel business. Doing this makes your travel tax-deductible! As long as you're doing it the right way. Remember, some businesses have more deductible benefits than others.

Here are a few additional considerations for choosing a home-based business. Is there a market for the product or service being sold/represented? Does the product/service have true consumer value? Does your product, good, service, or opportunity have serious competition, or are you involved with a category creator or disruptor?

Is the marketing system simple and duplicatable? Is the compensation proposal fair and lucrative? Is there a supportive team of partners and mentors available?

I would be remiss not to mention Real Estate Investing as it has, arguably, created more millionaires than anything else. Also in that arena is the rental market. There are huge profits in domestic rentals; however, there are also phenomenal opportunities in the foreign rental market as well. Do you believe it would be beneficial to do a little research?

Again, I mention the Living Benefit of life insurance has proven to be an excellent long-term investment. Why? Because it's your money. You can borrow against it and use that money to fund a passive and residual endeavor. You also have the choice to pay it back to yourself or not. Warrants looking into, don't you think?

Regardless of which home-based or online business you choose, after you do your due diligence, of course, the key to increasing your tax deductions with a home-based or online business is documentation. Documentation beats Conversation every time.

According to the professionals, you want to do and document specific activities to make your business IRS-compliant. This is a more detailed topic, and I am not a tax professional. However, this book has referenced resources available to guide you on this subject.

That said, remember, it is necessary to consistently do the Daily Business Building Activities (D.B.B.A.) to warrant or justify your business deductions and document them. This is very simple.

According to the professionals, you want to state your name, state your intentions of doing business and/or looking for customers, mention your product or service, ask for referrals, and leave them with contact information.

The following statement was developed to satisfy all guidelines to ensure documented activities are tax-deductible. Why? Because everywhere you go, you meet people. You have to be a walking advertisement for your business, and in doing so, your everyday activities can now help increase your financial bottom line. Now, you can turn some of your everyday activities into Daily Business Building Activities by using this one concept.

I call that statement an Income-Producing Conversation. It goes like this…

"Hello, I realize you don't know me from Adam/Alice. I'm (State your name). *However, I can always use more business and referrals.* (While handing them a business card) *Do you know anyone who wants to* (Mention the benefit of your product, good, or service) *make money on the internet, or would just like to know how to pay less taxes?"*

Saying this one statement while handing the prospect a business card or website is what we call the beginning of an Income-Producing Conversation, as it satisfies your attempt to gain or produce income, potentially making whatever activity you're currently doing a tax-deductible business expense.

"The Daily Business Building Activities are rooted

in the Income-Producing Conversation..."

Let's talk about the Income-Producing Conversation. This book is going to, once and for all, break it down to the bare bones. We have all hesitated in one conversation or another because we just didn't feel confident in our ability to conversate at that moment in time.

The Daily Business Building Activities are rooted in the Income-Producing Conversation, so let's cover them simultaneously. Since most people like to travel, let's say we have an online business in the travel industry as an example. Of course, it could be any type of business, but we'll use travel for the sake of ease in this section. Feel free to substitute your business or future business in place of "travel."

As we move about through our lives, we have opportunities to meet and greet others. Many people feel uncomfortable speaking with others. No longer does anyone have to feel uncomfortable when speaking to others. Here are some questions and answers with examples of proven successful responses of exactly what to say when you engage new acquaintances during a conversation so you can speak with complete confidence.

"Hello, how are you?"
I am wonderful, thank you. I realize you don't know me from Adam/Alice. I'm (State your name). *However, I can always use more business and referrals.*

(While handing them a business card) *Do you know anyone who wants to travel, make money on the internet, or would just like to know how to pay less taxes?* (Book Exposure)

"Hello, how are you today?"

I am wonderful, thank you. (While you're handing them a business card). *I am* (State your name). *Would you happen to know anyone who would like to travel at wholesale prices? I ask because I'm always looking for more customers and referrals. When would you have time to check out the website?* (Book Exposure)

During a Conversation.

Hey, if I told you that you could go to an online website and see wholesale travel prices rather than continue to pay the marked-up retail prices of Priceline and Expedia, would you? Great. I'm (State your name), *and I'm always looking for more customers and referrals* (While you're handing them a business card). *When is a good time for you to check it out?* (Book Exposure)

"Yes, I know someone who would like to, but what do they have to do?"

They have to say exactly what I said. There is no selling or convincing or anything like that. It's simply finding people who either like to travel or vacation, want to make or save money, want to make money without having a second job, or just want to pay less money out in taxes. Make sense? (Book Exposure)

So, you get paid for handing me this card?

(Laugh a little) *No, Ma'am/Sir. The brief explanation is that I am part of a larger group that helps people all day, every day, to increase their financial awareness and income. By doing just what I did, which, as you can see, is simply handing out a business card and asking a few questions, I actually pay less taxes, which increases my take-home money. It's all very legal, moral, and ethical. Does that make more sense?* (Book Exposure)

"How much does it cost?"
Good question. If I told you that you could make an extra $300 per month if you spent $300 one time, would you do it? Okay, what if I said the cost varies because there are different choices available, like deciding how much you want to invest in stocks and bonds? Everyone is different, right? But that's getting ahead of ourselves. Somebody else explains all that stuff to everyone. I just invite people to listen to the specifics on a video. Am I wrong, you sound interested in hearing the specific details? (Book Exposure)

(Laugh a little) *Sir/Ma'am, you wouldn't believe me if I told you. Let me answer this way. Some people in our group are actually paid to travel and vacation because of the tax deductions involved. My best advice is for you to watch the video and check it out for yourself. Make sense?* (Book Exposure)

(Laugh a little) *Now, that's putting the cart before the horse. Cost doesn't matter if something has no value to you. Check it out for yourself. Watch the video; if you like what you hear, we'll go from there. Fair enough?* (Book Exposure)

"What is it?"

A situation that allows us to lower our taxes, enjoy tax-deductible travel, create income, and save money, all while letting somebody else do all of the hard work for us. We just have to invite people to take a look at a video. Sound good? (Book Exposure)

"What would I have to do?"
If you can play 'Follow the Leader,' then you will be able to allow people who have already had success to guide you to your own success. You earn while you learn. It's all mapped out for you; however, you have to see it for yourself. Make sense? (Book Exposure)

"It sounds too good to be true!"
I can understand how you'd feel that way; many have felt that way, too. The fact remains that what we do is legal, moral, and ethical, and these folks are helping more and more people every day. The question is, will you make time to see it for yourself? (Book Exposure)

For those in network marketing and/or affiliate marketing…

"Is it a pyramid?"
Of course it is, isn't every company? (Book Exposure)

Since all companies are pyramids, are you asking me if it's legal, moral, and ethical? (Book Exposure)

Since all companies are pyramids, are you asking me if it's a Ponzi scheme with no product? (Book Exposure)

Absolutely, or it would be called a JOB, wouldn't it? (Book Exposure)

How about you see the information for yourself and then decide? (Book Exposure)

I couldn't leave out my personal favorite: *Why do you like pyramids?* (Yes/No, does not matter) *Excellent, you'll love what we've got.* (Book Exposure)

I say, "You'll love what we've got" because I direct them to what they want. If they like network marketing, I refer them to the video that shows that side of the business. If they don't, then I refer them to the video that only talks about the product. Either way, they'll love what we've got.

This response was inspired by a very successful businessman, Ray. *I ran into a business group that caught my attention in a big way. It may just be a shot in the dark because I don't know if the timing is right for you or not, but I have found a group of people who help people like you and me make money online. Could you and your family use some additional money coming in without having to get an additional job? You should check it out for yourself. If you like it, great. If not, no big deal. Either way, we'll part friends, right?* (Book Exposure)

There are an unlimited number of ways to introduce your business, whatever it is.

Do you know four people who have been adversely affected by the pandemic/economy and could use some additional income if it did not interfere with what they are currently doing? (Book Exposure)

Do you know anyone who is trying to make money online and could use the resources of a group of people who can help them be successful online? (Book Exposure)

Hey friend. This may be a shot in the dark, but let me ask you a question. If I could introduce you to a team of people who help people like you and me change our financial bottom line, would you sit down and listen? (Book Exposure)

If I told you that you could lower the amount of taxes you pay, which increases your take-home pay, which will allow you to take your family on vacation with that same money, would you sit down and listen? (Book Exposure)

If I told you that you could use some of the tax money you're already paying and simply redirect it to, let's say, a dream vacation, a new car, or to get out of debt, would you sit down and listen? (Book Exposure)

For those in the N.F.L. Club who have a person who is real, available, and has had success.

Hey friend. I know we have done some things in the past that didn't work out the way we wanted, and now I have found out WHY it didn't work out. Turns out, it wasn't our fault. We didn't have a team full of resources to back us up. We didn't have somebody else doing all of the hard work for us. Well, the good news is that they actually exist. I think I found them. Actually, they found me. Awesome resources, I'm telling you. When can we watch the video together and see if it's the real deal? (Book Exposure)

Okay, you get the idea. There is a secret to it that makes it easy. It's a pattern. Choose any of the Opening Phrases, insert the Transitional Statement, and finish with an Ending Phrase, followed by a closing question. Remember always to include the Transitional Statement.

So, pick one from each category, forming the invitation appropriate for the situation—one from the Opening Phrases, insert the Transitional Statement, and then choose from the Ending Phrases. Then, ask the closing question.

Opening Phrases:
That's a great question; however…
I agree with you; however…
That's a valid concern; however…
Yes, I understand completely; however…

Transitional Statement:
…I would feel more comfortable if…

Ending Phases:
…You watched the short video.
…Went to the website.

…Met us for coffee.

…Attended the live Zoom.

Example:

That's a valid concern; however, I would feel more comfortable if you watched the short video. Sound good?

Booking the Exposure:

It's very simple. Don't overcomplicate this. It's an easy narrowing down effect of alternate closes. If they do not give you a specific time and date to complete your ending phrase, then use this technique. It's not pushy or forward in any way.

When would be a good time, Tuesday or Thursday? Morning or Evening? Before dinner or after dinner? Before lunch or after dinner? Use any TWO days or time frames.

After agreeing on a specific time, date, and place, you tell them that you are putting the appointment into your calendar to follow through with them at a specific time and date that you book with them.

Remember, these statements are designed to ensure you are not the bully type, brow-beating people into submission. This is not the way to success. On the opposite side of the coin, these statements allow you a shield of protection as well.

> *"...do not perform phone presentations or get tricked*
> *into submitting to sidewalk seminars."*

Be aware that some people will push and insist on getting information from you now. They will just keep grilling you until you give in and answer all of their questions right then and there. They believe that they can make a decision at that time without all the details. Don't do it.

Do not play twenty questions with your prospects. That very rarely works. Simply use your tools and training to expose them to ALL the information that they will need to make an informed decision. Unless you are trained to do so, DO NOT, under ANY circumstances, explain the specifics of your product, goods, service, or opportunity!

For their own good, do not perform phone presentations or get tricked into submitting to sidewalk seminars. There is no success in falling into that trap. You are going to want them to duplicate what you are doing, so don't give in. Walk away and re-approach them again some other time.

Have unshakable POSTURE. I'm sure you believe your company or opportunity is offering something that has value. Whether they are new to your industry or seasoned veterans, they have never seen what you are offering them at that moment. Similar? Maybe. Identical? Doubt it. You are doing great, wonderful, and unprecedented things, so have posture. And remember, your product, good, service, or opportunity is NOT for everyone.

Correct me if I'm wrong. It is *not* for people who *cannot* or *will not* follow instructions. Your opportunity is *not* for people who are *not* team players. It is *not* for people who already know everything. It is *not* for people who are *not* willing to work for their success. It is *not* for people who feel they are entitled to spillover.

However, your product, good, service, or opportunity *is* for people who *can* see the value of what you're offering. Go through your proper steps according to your training, and crush the 80/20 rule.

Speaking of the 80/20 rule, there is something else I haven't shared. Although I previously mentioned it, I hesitate to go into depth with this training, in this book. I was just going to touch on it. Why? Because it is so simple that it is overwhelming for people who have not personally developed to this level yet. Well, here it is in depth.

"It creates success beyond people's wildest imaginations."

The challenge is that I've done it. I have friends and colleagues who have done it. It works. It creates success beyond people's wildest imaginations. But it's too simple. It's as simple as Believe, Learn, Practice, and Teach. It's so simple that people don't believe it. It's what I call the 10-4 Marketing Program.

It does not matter what your product, good, service, or opportunity is. The marketing numbers hash out the same. As long as you are offering something of value—that involves people receiving a substantial enough reward for referring others to that value—then the numbers will illustrate how successful such an endeavor can be. Let's take a look.

The 10-4 Marketing Program illustrates what results can come from such a simple thing as performing this Daily Business Building Activity (D.B.B.A.)

Can you do the Daily Business Building Activity (D.B.B.A.) of asking this Income-Producing Conversation question?

"Hello, I realize you don't know me from Adam/Alice. I'm (State your name). *However, I can always use more business and referrals.* (While handing them a business card) *Do you know anyone who wants to* (Mention the benefit of

your product, good, or service) *make money on the internet, or would just like to know how to pay less taxes?"*

Can you make 10 Contacts per day for 6 days? That's it! Use the seventh day to relax and meditate. Here are the numbers if you can. You don't have to go headhunting or bother your family and friends. It's just a conversation like any other conversation. Just properly invite people to look at what you have and let universal laws take over.

THE 10-4 MARKETING PROGRAM

Make 10 Contacts/day X 6 days = 60 Contacts X 4 weeks = 240 Contacts/Invites

10 Contacts per day times 6 days a week equals 60 properly made
Contacts. Multiply that by 4 weeks, which equals 240 properly made
Contacts or Invites to look at your product, good, service, or

THE 10-4 MARKETING PROGRAM

Make 10 Contacts/day X 6 days = 60 Contacts X 4 weeks = 240 Contacts/Invites

Don't Look   80%   /\   20%   Look

192   48

opportunity.

From the 240 Contact/Invites, we can eliminate 80% or 192 people; they lied. They said they would go look at the video or meet you for

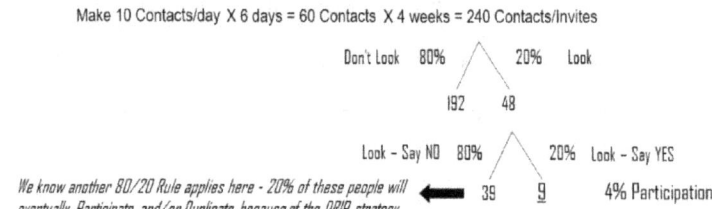

THE 10-4 MARKETING PROGRAM

Make 10 Contacts/day X 6 days = 60 Contacts X 4 weeks = 240 Contacts/Invites

Don't Look   80%   20%   Look

192   48

Look – Say NO   80%   20%   Look – Say YES

We know another 80/20 Rule applies here - 20% of these people will eventually Participate and/or Duplicate because of the DRIP strategy.   ⬅   39   9   4% Participation

coffee or whatever. They said they would and didn't. The remaining 20%, the 48 people who said they would look, actually did go and look. We are excited! We think that we are going to work with or do business with these 48 people—we're not.

We have to apply the 80/20 rule to this group of 48 Contact/Invites. As you can see, 80% or 39 Contacts/Invites look at what you're offering but will say "No" at that moment. However, a marketing concept called the Drip Strategy will yield another 80/20 rule from the 39 who said "No." The majority of this group does not know whether to say yes or no, so they sit on the sidelines, watching. Eventually, with the Drip Strategy, they will see the train moving and jump on the bandwagon. It's a wonderful boost whenever it does happen, depending on momentum.

The remaining 9 Contacts/Invites, or 20%, will participate. These 9 Contacts/Invites will all have some level of positive compliance: to join your team, invest in your idea, partner with you, or just be a great customer. The math tells us that these 9 Contacts/Invites are 4% of the whole—the 240 initial Contacts/Invites. To be clear, that's just 4% Participation.

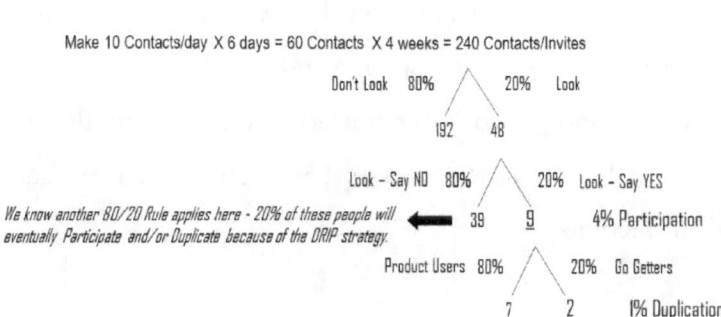

THE 10-4 MARKETING PROGRAM

Make 10 Contacts/day X 6 days = 60 Contacts X 4 weeks = 240 Contacts/Invites

Don't Look 80%   20% Look

192   48

Look – Say NO 80%   20% Look – Say YES

We know another 80/20 Rule applies here - 20% of these people will   39   9   4% Participation
eventually Participate and/or Duplicate because of the DRIP strategy.

Product Users 80%   20% Go Getters

7   2   1% Duplication

To ensure that you understand how low these numbers are, I'm going to apply the 80/20 rule again—yes, again. If we apply the 80/20 rule to the remaining 9 Contacts/Invites, then we have 7 Contacts/Invites who will be supportive and play a major role as product users, but they are not the go-getters. They are not the one percenters, the duplicators. That honor belongs to the remaining 20%, the 2 Contact/Invites.

These are your major players. These are the people who are as hungry as you. They will duplicate your efforts since you have success to show for your efforts. Since you now have low-hanging fruit, they will follow you or partner with you. They will multiply you. To be clear, that's just 1% Duplication.

Oh, but wait. Do you realize what's being illustrated here? Look at the numbers. People lie, numbers don't. According to the 80/20 rule, if you can simply make a statement **properly** Contacting or Inviting 10 people per day for 6 days for 4 weeks, then you will have a total of 9 people involved with you and two willing to duplicate what you are doing. Again, that's 4% Participation and only 1% Duplication. If your performance ratios at work were this low, you'd be terminated. However, as I said, this is not a job. This is creating Passive and Residual Income.

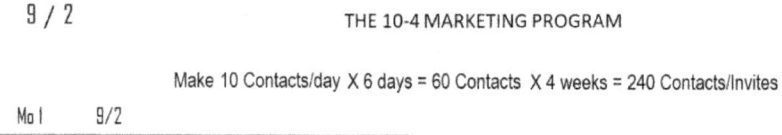

9 / 2   THE 10-4 MARKETING PROGRAM

Make 10 Contacts/day X 6 days = 60 Contacts X 4 weeks = 240 Contacts/Invites

Mo I   9/2

This graph is representative of your first month of productivity. You brought on 9, of which 2 will duplicate. It's all about properly making the Contacts or Invites. As you build a large team, the numbers get crazy.

But remember that no one is doing any more than what has already been detailed. We do the Daily Business Building Activities or make

proper Contacts/Invites, document our expenditures, and develop Passive and Residual Income. In doing so, we teach others to do the same.

Brace yourself. These are the results of doing that one-month cycle of 10X6X4=240, creating the 9 who Participate and 2 who Duplicate.

9 / 2   THE 10-4 MARKETING PROGRAM

Make 10 Contacts/day X 6 days = 60 Contacts X 4 weeks = 240 Contacts/Invites

Mo 1	9/2
Mo 2	18/3
	9/2
	9/2
	18/4
	/\
	3.6

In Month 2, your two go-getters are going to Duplicate. By doing exactly what you did, they will yield their own 9/2 each. That's 18 new people that have now come under your business umbrella. If we looked at each of their 9s and 2s individually and simply added them together, we would end with 18 Participating and 4 Duplicating. Instead, let's apply yet another 80/20 rule and decide there is no 3.6 of a person and round down to 3 Contacts/Invites willing to Duplicate. As you can see, I am dumbing these numbers down at every opportunity, and they will still end up astronomically high. So, that leaves us with 18 new Participants, of which 3 will Duplicate.

You continue to do your Daily Business Building Activities and documenting so as to continue reducing your own tax liability. Let's look at what Month 3 has to offer.

9 / 2

THE 10-4 MARKETING PROGRAM

Make 10 Contacts/day X 6 days = 60 Contacts X 4 weeks = 240 Contacts/Invites

Mo 1	9/2	
Mo 2	18/3	9/2
Mo 3	27/5	
	9/2	
	9/2	
	9/2	
	27/6	
	/\	
	5.4	

In Month 2, your first group of 9/2 introduced their own individual groups of 9/2 each, and as previously stated, you continue to do the D.B.B.A. introducing a second group of 9/2 Contacts/Invites. As we continue to use the 80/20 rule, in Month 3, the 3 go-getters of the 18/3 will produce a 9/2 each individually. That's 27 Participants and 6 Duplicators being reduced to 27 and 5.

9 / 2   THE 10-4 MARKETING PROGRAM

Make 10 Contacts/day X 6 days = 60 Contacts X 4 weeks = 240 Contacts/Invites

Mo 1	9/2		
Mo 2	18/3	9/2	
Mo 3	27/5	18/3	
	9/2	9/2	
	9/2	9/2	
	9/2	18/4	
	27/6	∧	
	∧	3.6	
	5.4		

You can see the pattern; 9/2s create 18/3s and 18/3s create 27/5s. As we continue, you will see unbelievable numbers. These numbers represent a simple Contacting and Inviting method backed by powers of influence and persuasion. And remember, we're only talking 4% Participation and 1% Duplication.

9 / 2   THE 10-4 MARKETING PROGRAM

Make 10 Contacts/day X 6 days = 60 Contacts X 4 weeks = 240 Contacts/Invites

Mo 1	9/2		
Mo 2	18/3	9/2	
Mo 3	27/5	18/3	9/2

Completing Month 3 is watching Duplication in process. Remember, you are not responsible for all of these numbers. You are just doing your own D.B.B.A. and introducing a group of 9/2 each month. Your go-getters own their own business and are doing the same as you do. They are Duplicating you in creating Passive and Residual Income by introducing 9/2s of their own each month.

9 / 2   THE 10-4 MARKETING PROGRAM

Make 10 Contacts/day X 6 days = 60 Contacts X 4 weeks = 240 Contacts/Invites

Mo 1	9/2			
Mo 2	18/3	9/2		
Mo 3	27/5	18/3	9/2	
Mo 4	45/9	27/5	18/3	9/2

Moving forward, notice the pattern of predictable success. These numbers are not magical. They are simply the result of treating yourself like a business by inviting others to take a look at a video or other presentation method. It's not a question of whether they say yes or no because you are doing the D.B.B.A., therefore creating tax-deductible business expenses for yourself, which will allow you to start keeping your own money in your own pocket. So, you have already profited and have nothing to lose. Simply continue to Contact and Invite and let the 80/20 rule do the rest.

9 / 2   THE 10-4 MARKETING PROGRAM

Make 10 Contacts/day X 6 days = 60 Contacts X 4 weeks = 240 Contacts/Invites

Mo 1	9/2					
Mo 2	18/3	9/2				
Mo 3	27/5	18/3	9/2			
Mo 4	45/9	27/5	18/3	9/2		
Mo 5	81/16	45/9	27/5	18/3	9/2	
Mo 6	144/28	81/16	45/9	27/5	18/3	9/2

Jumping to Month 6, you can see the predictable pattern. In Month 1, 9 people partnered with you. In Month 2, a total of 27 partnered with you. In Month 3, 54 new people entered your space. Each month will grow exponentially because one percenters *multiply* value to you; they don't just *add* value to you. Okay, let's get into some unbelievable numbers.

9 / 2   THE 10-4 MARKETING PROGRAM

Make 10 Contacts/day X 6 days = 60 Contacts X 4 weeks = 240 Contacts/Invites

Mo 1	9/2											
Mo 2	18/3	9/2										
Mo 3	27/5	18/3	9/2									
Mo 4	45/9	27/5	18/3	9/2								
Mo 5	81/16	45/9	27/5	18/3	9/2							
Mo 6	144/28	81/16	45/9	27/5	18/3	9/2						
Mo 7	252/50	144/28	81/16	45/9	27/5	18/3	9/2					
Mo 8	450/90	252/50	144/28	81/16	45/9	27/5	18/3	9/2				
Mo 9	810/162	450/90	252/50	144/28	81/16	45/9	27/5	18/3	9/2			
Mo 10	1,458/291	810/162	450/90	252/50	144/28	81/16	45/9	27/5	18/3	9/2		
Mo 11	2,619/523	1,458/291	810/162	450/90	252/50	144/28	81/16	45/9	27/5	18/3	9/2	
Mo 12	4,707/841	2,619/523	1,458/291	810/162	450/90	252/50	144/28	81/16	45/9	27/5	18/3	9/2

After just 1 year, these are the numbers under your umbrella. I told you they were unbelievable. It's simple, not easy. If it were easy, everyone would be doing it. You can see that even with the 80/20 rule being applied many times to reduce numbers, the powerful results of exponential growth cannot be denied. Exponential growth cannot be stopped. It's like a snowball rolling downhill. It can only be stopped by inactivity. Let's total these up and see what we have after just 1 year.

9 / 2   THE 10-4 MARKETING PROGRAM

Make 10 Contacts/day X 6 days = 60 Contacts X 4 weeks = 240 Contacts/Invites

Mo 1	9/2	=	9											
Mo 2	18/3	9/2	=	27										
Mo 3	27/5	18/3	9/2	=	54									
Mo 4	45/9	27/5	18/3	9/2	=	99								
Mo 5	81/16	45/9	27/5	18/3	9/2	=	180							
Mo 6	144/28	81/16	45/9	27/5	18/3	9/2	=	324						
Mo 7	252/50	144/28	81/16	45/9	27/5	18/3	9/2	=	576					
Mo 8	450/90	252/50	144/28	81/16	45/9	27/5	18/3	9/2	=	1,026				
Mo 9	810/162	450/90	252/50	144/28	81/16	45/9	27/5	18/3	9/2	=	1,836			
Mo 10	1,458/291	810/162	450/90	252/50	144/28	81/16	45/9	27/5	18/3	9/2	=	3,294		
Mo 11	2,619/523	1,458/291	810/162	450/90	252/50	144/28	81/16	45/9	27/5	18/3	9/2	=	5,813	
Mo 12	4,707/941	2,619/523	1,458/291	810/162	450/90	252/50	144/28	81/16	45/9	27/5	18/3	9/2	=	10,620

These are the totals of the people entering your umbrella each month. Can you believe 1,836 people entering into your space, not in 9 months, but just in Month 9? Most are UN-ABLE to see themselves have this kind of success because they haven't had the training contained in this book. They can't see themselves being this successful in their mind, so they never get to see it in real-time. Take a look at this next mind-blowing graph.

THE 10-4 MARKETING PROGRAM

Make 10 Contacts/day X 6 days = 60 Contacts X 4 weeks = 240 Contacts/Invites

Mo 1	9/2	=	9	=	9												
Mo 2	18/3	9/2	=	27	=	36											
Mo 3	27/5	18/3	9/2	=	54	=	90										
Mo 4	45/9	27/5	18/3	9/2	=	99	=	189									
Mo 5	81/16	45/9	27/5	18/3	9/2	=	180	=	369								
Mo 6	144/28	81/16	45/9	27/5	18/3	9/2	=	324	=	693							
Mo 7	252/50	144/28	81/16	45/9	27/5	18/3	9/2	=	576	=	1,269						
Mo 8	450/90	252/50	144/28	81/16	45/9	27/5	18/3	9/2	=	1,026	=	2,295					
Mo 9	810/162	450/90	252/50	144/28	81/16	45/9	27/5	18/3	9/2	=	1,836	=	4,131				
Mo 10	1,458/291	810/162	450/90	252/50	144/28	81/16	45/9	27/5	18/3	9/2	=	3,294	=	7,425			
Mo 11	2,619/523	1,458/291	810/162	450/90	252/50	144/28	81/16	45/9	27/5	18/3	9/2	=	5,813	=	13,238		
Mo 12	4,707/941	2,619/523	1,458/291	810/162	450/90	252/50	144/28	81/16	45/9	27/5	18/3	9/2	=	10,620	=	23,858	

In conclusion, 9 people entered your umbrella in Month 1. Add that 9 to the 27 that entered in Month 2, and you have a total of 36 people involved. Add that 36 to the 54 that entered Month 3, and now there are 90 Contacts/Invites being leveraged. Add that 90 to the 99 in Month 4, and there are now 189. Continue the math, and you will have a total of 23,858 Contacts/Invites who have joined somewhere under your umbrella. And that's taking the 20% of every group continually. Amazing, isn't it?

9 / 2

Make 10 Contacts/day X 6 days = 60 Contacts X 4 weeks = 240 Contacts/Invites

Mo 1	9/2
Mo 2	18/3
Mo 3	27/5
Mo 4	45/9
Mo 5	81/16
Mo 6	144/28
Mo 7	252/50
Mo 8	450/90
Mo 9	810/162
Mo 10	1,458/291
Mo 11	2,619/523
Mo 12	4,707/941

After just one year, based on the ridiculously scaled down numbers of 9 Participating and 2 Duplicating, that's 4% Participation and less than 1% Duplication, from just 240 properly performed Contacts or Invites, without ANYONE doing ANYTHING beyond their initial one-month of 9/2 D.B.B.A.

What results does the 10-4 Marketing Program produce?

I know these numbers are completely unbelievable for many of you as you have not yet assimilated the skill sets shared in this book. So, let's do this. Let's wipe out all activity past each person's first month. That means we're getting rid of all activity after Month 1. Let's just wipe it out. You only did the D.B.B.A. to bring onboard 9/2. Those 2 only worked 1 month and brought in their 9/2 each. Continuing to apply the 80/20 rule, and, of course, the results are still staggering!

So, after 1 year, based on the ridiculously scaled-down numbers of 9 Participating and 2 Duplicating, which is only 4% Participation and 1% Duplication, from just 240 **properly** performed Contacts/Invites, without anyone doing anything beyond their one-month of 9/2 D.B.B.A.

What results does the 10-4 Marketing Program produce?

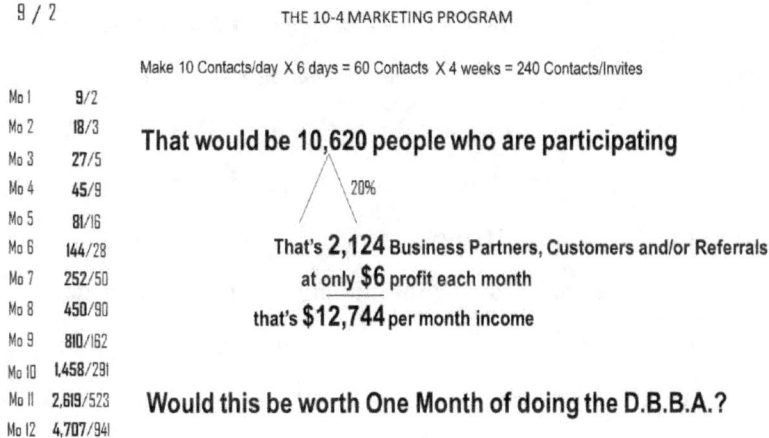

THE 10-4 MARKETING PROGRAM

Make 10 Contacts/day X 6 days = 60 Contacts X 4 weeks = 240 Contacts/Invites

Mo 1	9/2
Mo 2	18/3
Mo 3	27/5
Mo 4	45/9
Mo 5	81/16
Mo 6	144/28
Mo 7	252/50
Mo 8	450/90
Mo 9	810/162
Mo 10	1,458/291
Mo 11	2,619/523
Mo 12	4,707/941

9 / 2

That would be 10,620 people who are participating

20%

That's **2,124** Business Partners, Customers and/or Referrals
at only **$6** profit each month
that's **$12,744** per month income

Would this be worth One Month of doing the D.B.B.A.?

You would have a total of 10,620 people under your umbrella. You should know my style well enough now to know that I will apply YET ANOTHER 80/20 rule to the 10,620, leaving us with 2,124 Contacts/Invites on your team. If you only profited $6 from each, that would produce a passive and residual of $12,744 monthly!

Remember, these numbers are ridiculously reduced to ensure your belief. Your Residual Income, your financial freedom, and your peace of mind, are only a Daily Business Building Activity away from reality.

"With this book, you have the basics of creating a passive and residual income for you and your family."

The trainings that have been converted so that they can be shared in this book are extremely powerful. The techniques are proven. Millions of people use these techniques and strategies every day in some form. I dare say very few understand how they all fit together to create the best versions of ourselves. This book gives you the basics of creating a Passive and Residual Income for you and your family through personal development.

What would have changed or been handled differently if you had already created these additional incomes when we were all locked down for COVID-19? Are you going to create passive and residual income before another pandemic, war, or social crisis locks the world down?

Just suppose another pandemic does occur; let's call it SEERS, or a pandemic-size resurgence of Marburg virus disease, or a 2017 Equifax size data breach of the US Government. How about something equivalent? Something like digital currencies meets AI meets corrupt government, resulting in a depression worse than the Great Depression. What will you do then?

If having an online business saves you money in taxes and/or can make you a few hundred or thousands of dollars online, do you think it makes sense to create additional streams of income, especially Passive and Residual Income?

It is a fact that 95% to 97% of the millions of people who enter the business of Relationship Marketing, fail to create the sustainable residual income they work so hard and long to create. By the way, this is the crux of where the 5%'ers come from. Do you want to be a five percenter?

When this question was asked of me, I replied, "Absolutely!" Then, it was explained to me that I needed to stop creating Linear Income and start creating Passive and Residual Income. Being honest, I told my business mentor that I was not aware of the difference between the incomes mentioned. Here's how he broke it down for me.

Linear Income is income that you have to physically be present to create it, like a job. Passive Income is income you can create without physically being on-site, like having an automated online store. Then there is Residual Income. This is income you create that continues to come in after you have done the work once, like writing a hit record.

Additionally, there is the one-two combo punch, Passive & Residual Income. This is income where you do not have to be there as the work has already been done, and it pays you in perpetuity—even after you're physically gone.

I realized I needed to learn how to create Passive Income, Residual Income, and Passive & Residual Income simply because the odds were against me to live a satisfied life and enjoy a successful retirement with only Linear Income.

It was explained to me that I needed to be out of the rat race so I could reach my full potential. This is how I was introduced to Robert Kiyosaki and his Rich Dad Poor Dad series, including his training on the Cashflow Quadrant.

This was previously referenced in this book as the Work Status category. You can see E, S, B, and I in the illustration. The E stands for Employee. The S stands for Specialists (Doctor, Lawyer, Self-employed). The B stands for Big Business (500 or more employees). The I stands for Investor. I revisit this topic to share one major key to success. We need to be on the right side of the quadrant to create Passive and Residual Income. If you doubt, purchase the Kiyosaki board game called "Cashflow 101." You'll learn more than you can imagine.

The Internet has provided each of us with the opportunity to create passive and residual income because we can experience ubiquity. Ubiquity is having the capacity to be everywhere at once. As was explained to me, as long as you work for another person, you are making another person rich, richer, or wealthy.

More importantly, I want you to understand that your job MUST make a profit off your work, or they can't afford to pay you. That's why, with a job, you will always be paid what the POSITION is worth, not what YOU are worth.

If you can find your way from the left side of the quadrant to the right side, you will have the opportunity to live the lifestyle you desire. Then, you will have the opportunity to spend more than a few dollars to make more than a few dimes. Then, you will have the opportunity to leave your chosen legacy for future generations.

Please believe you can do this at any age; however, the earlier you start, the sooner you can leave the traditional workforce and enjoy life on your terms. Regardless of your age, this is also known as retirement—retirement from the traditional workforce.

"...we base our decisions on
"either what we have faith for
or what we have fear in."

In closing, I dare say this book has provided you with enough information to help you on your journey. Regardless of your current station in life, whether you're just making the decision to change your stars or well into your chosen life path, you now have more information for your next steps. With these skills, knowledge, and newfound belief, you can now achieve anything that you truly believe that you can achieve.

Here is where I found my spiritual permission.

> *"18 Behold, here is what I have seen to be good and fitting: to eat and drink, and to find enjoyment in all the labor in which he labors under the sun during the few days of his life which God gives him—for this is his [allotted] reward. 19 Also, every man to whom God has given riches and possessions, He has also given the power and ability to enjoy them and to receive [this as] his [allotted] portion and to rejoice in his labor—this is the gift of God [to him]. 20 For he will not often consider the [troubled] days of his life, because God keeps occupied and focused on the joy of his heart [and the tranquility of God indwells him]."*
> (Ecclesiastes 5:18-20 AMP)

The energy within us keeps us in tune with what is natural. It is natural to seek success, to endure the trials and tribulations that come with living a human life. In this, we are expected to be more than a conqueror and enjoy overwhelming victory, says Romans 8:37 (AMP).

We have the ability to overcome. We've been given the choice to seek out the strength and courage to learn and persevere through any kind of challenge while striving for our goals and dreams.

The topic of belief in oneself always brings me back to a sermon I heard delivered in love by Dr. Kevin A. Williams. I believe it was titled "Anointed for Next." To paraphrase, he talked about not hating the challenges we face in life. Those very challenges are in our lives so we can personally develop through those trials, which prepare us for the difficulties ahead. That preparation, or challenging time in our life, is exactly what we needed at that time to develop the knowledge, discipline, and courage we'll need to be successful in our assignment.

He continued to explain that God thinks differently than we do. He thinks differently about us than we think about ourselves. This is supported in Isaiah, which states, "[8]For my thoughts are not your thoughts, neither are your ways my ways, saith the Lord. [9]For as the heavens are higher than the earth, so are my ways higher than your ways, and my thoughts than your thoughts. (Isaiah 55:8-9 KJV)

Why? Because He is omnipotent and thinks way beyond our earthly limitations. When we think about ourselves, we are basing those thoughts on what we remember about our past, what we remember about our experiences, and either what we have faith for or fear in, when it comes to our future. Please allow me to say that again. In respect to our future, Pastor Williams said, we base our decisions on "either what we have **faith for** or what we have **fear in**."

We can choose to strive forward with conviction because we believe we have an assignment or purpose for our lives, or we can succumb to fear and self-doubt. Our God knows us better than we know ourselves and knows what we need to go through to develop to the point where we can handle our life assignment, as referenced in Romans 5:3 (KJV).

Since we are made up of our experiences, and what we learn from them, these are the ingredients needed to make the next steps in our life journey. This is how we build a foundation of growth from which we encounter tribulations, which develops patience, which teaches experience, and which gives us hope, "and hope maketh not ashamed" (Romans 5:5 KJV).

I'm sure you have realized that if you invest the time, effort, and money into your personal development, the rewards could multiply exponentially, in your not-to-distant future.

So, I pose this question again, as I did in the beginning: Are you willing to spend a dollar to make a dime? If so, then you now have a clear path to elevate your game, to invest in yourself, to invest in yourself for your future generations, and to enjoy a lifestyle far beyond your own perceived ceiling.

Prepare yourself for the trials and tribulations that come with personal development. You will find yourself looking at the world just a bit differently. You will see opportunities where others just see problems. You will make decisions rather than let others make decisions for you.

This happens when we say things similar to, "You decide," "Whatever you want," "Anything is fine," or, my personal favorite, "Surprise me." When we make statements of this sort, we are giving away our decision-making power. The decision is made for us. One way or another, the decision will be made. The question is, did you make the decision, or was it made for you?

One word of caution. As you begin to grow, some of the people closest to you will not understand, and your relationship with them may suffer a bit. You will have the choice to keep that relationship or not. Remember, to be understood by the 2%, you are sometimes misunderstood by the 98%.

This author recommends you take a serious look at the material in this book and read it again, if necessary. Read it out loud with dramatic voice inflection if you have to. But whatever you do, Believe it, Learn it, Practice it, and Teach it!

We hope you enjoy your Riches Within Reach as you implement A Retirement Cure! As my friend Maria would say, "Make the rest of your life the best of your life."

And just so you know, this author believes in YOU.

Thank you, and Congratulations on taking "your next step."

References

1- https://www.sutori.com/en/item/almost-exactly-nine-months-after-world-war-ii-ended-the-cry-of-the-baby-was-he-407d

2- https://www.tonyrobbins.com/mind-meaning/how-to-reprogram-your-mind/#:~:text=The%20subconscious%20mind%20goes%20beyond,what%20to%20store%20for%20later.

3- https://www.biblegateway.com/passage/?search=Ecclesiastes%205&version=NIV,KJV

4- https://www.globenewswire.com/en/news-release/2022/03/02/2395201/28124/en/Impacts-of-the-Baby-Boomer-Generation-has-on-Several-Global-Markets-2022-Market-Research-Report.html

5- https://www.fool.com/research/average-retirement-savings/

6- https://www.gobankingrates.com/retirement/planning/jaw-dropping-stats-state-retirement-america/

7- https://www.federalreserve.gov/publications/2021-economic-well-being-of-us-households-in-2020-retirement.htm

8- https://www.financialsamurai.com/age-people-retire-america/

9- https://www.cnbc.com/2021/09/14/these-policy-changes-are-needed-to-help-americans-retire-experts-say.html

10- https://www.investopedia.com/terms/1/80-20-rule.asp

11- https://asana.com/resources/pareto-principle-80-20-rule

12- https://www.forbes.com/sites/kevinkruse/2016/03/07/80-20-rule/?sh=1efd829c3814

13- https://www.lollydaskal.com/leadership/story-everybody-somebody-anybody-nobody/

14- https://www.collinsdictionary.com/us/dictionary/english/persuasion

15- https://www.collinsdictionary.com/us/dictionary/english/influence

16- https://www.collinsdictionary.com/us/dictionary/english/leadership

17- 21 Irrefutable Laws of Leadership by Dr John C. Maxwell

18- Power Persuasion : Using Hypnotic Influence in Life, Love and Business by Danek S. Kaus and David R. Barron

19- https://www.booksamillion.com/p/Power-Persuasion/Danek-S-Kaus/9781931741521?id=8140810130108

20- The One Sentence Persuasion Course by Blair Warren

21- https://www.dictionary.com/browse/goal

22- https://www.chicagochristiancounseling.org/files/NL14_01assertiveness.pdf

23- https://dictionary.cambridge.org/dictionary/english/nominalization

www.ingramcontent.com/pod-product-compliance
Lightning Source LLC
Chambersburg PA
CBHW072159290526
45794CB00004B/1578